Prais
A Survivor's

"The narrator in these remarkable stories speaks with two voices. At times we hear the voice of the teenager Felicia Bornstein, as she describes her life in the Pabianice Ghetto and her imprisonment in Auschwitz. This is a voice of loss, anger, and immeasurable sadness. And we hear the voice of adult Felicia Bornstein Lubliner, as she looks back on the terrible events of her youth, trying to find meaning in them. Hers is a voice of hope. With both voices, the narrator tells tales of courage and of faith: the courage to bear witness; faith that someone will listen."

— Kenneth Ehrlich, Rabbi and Former Dean, Hebrew Union College – Jewish Institute of Religion

"As historians and educators, the most impactful way to teach history is from those who lived through it. This book allows us to see inside the strength of one woman to survive the horrors of the Holocaust, and her struggle with the trauma for the rest of her life. These stories put a human voice to the number of six million Jews that were lost. Although it is impossible to fully comprehend what living through the Holocaust entailed, Felicia's vivid descriptions provide the reader an opportunity to construct an image and feel her emotions.

Her explanation of the selection process conveyed confusion and chaos, making clear that there was no time to think, to react, or to resist in the moment. Yet, Felicia's story is about resistance and her will to survive. Her stories challenge our understanding of what the Holocaust looked like and the experiences of the people who lived through it."

— Amanda Solomon, Manager of Museum and Holocaust Education, & Shannon Fleischman, Educator, Oregon Jewish Museum and Center for Holocaust Education

"Irving Lubliner's compilation of his mother's stories is an act of love. For the last three years, he has read six of the unpublished pieces aloud to my remedial and college-prep English classes. Powerful! Unforgettable! Heart-wrenching! The imagery will stir you and tears will flow."

— BETSY BISHOP, Teacher, Ashland High School

"In just a few pages these stories vivify the horror of the Holocaust and the redemption of the human will. Felicia Lubliner makes us realize in *Only Hope* that the spark of life cannot be extinguished even in the darkest of times."

— DENNIS M. READ, Professor Emeritus of English, Denison University

"If you ever visit Auschwitz, you most likely will find yourself deep in thought—trying to make sense of the magnitude of the camp and the atrocities that occurred within its electrified barbed wire. How do we wrap our heads around the brutality? How can we possibly understand what went on here? Felicia Lubliner's personal stories, *Only Hope: A Survivor's Stories of the Holocaust*, enable the reader to grapple with these questions. Stories of human beings—families, children, spouses, parents and friends—are recollected in great detail to reflect both the repugnant and the mundane existence inside the camp. Through a personal, unique and diverse lens, Felicia Lubliner conveys the raw emotional experience of a young woman trapped in the unimaginable depths of despair, yet through whose written words we find hope. Felicia Lubliner's *Only Hope* guides the reader through a Holocaust story that is much deeper than a number—6,000,000—giving us a human touch in the midst of inhumanity."

— DENNIS J. EISNER, Senior Rabbi, Peninsula Temple Beth El

"What would you have done? A simple question asked in countless contexts. Add the word "Auschwitz" and it becomes a searing, soul-searching challenge. In her compelling book, *Only Hope*, Holocaust survivor Felicia Bornstein Lubliner asks the reader to travel back in time, to follow her into the Nazi death camp, and to wrestle with this question, just as she did when faced with that reality."

— GEORGE CONKLIN, Project Director,
Worldwide Faith News, National Council of Churches

"*Only Hope* by Felicia Lubliner is a valuable addition to the autobiographical accounts of the dark chapter of the Holocaust. A gifted writer, she weaves beauty and humanity into her writing without sparing the grim details of the horrors of Auschwitz and the Holocaust. We owe our thanks to her son, Irving, for preserving his mother's words and sharing them with the rest of us now."

— SUSANNE SEVEREID, Author and host,
Emmy Award-winning PBS documentary,
C.A.N.D.L.E.S.: The Story of the Mengele Twins

"The Nazis attempted to strip their victims of every ounce of their humanity. They cut off their hair, gave them rags to wear, separated them from their loved ones, and replaced their names with a number tattooed on their arm. These stories stand as proof that the Nazis failed in their goal and in the end only degraded themselves. Felicia Lubliner shows us that the Jews did not submit meekly, but instead used every weapon at their disposal to fight back and thus maintain their own dignity. They are a gripping reminder of the power of the human spirit."

— ROBERT SCHUG,
Middle School Teacher, Bentley School

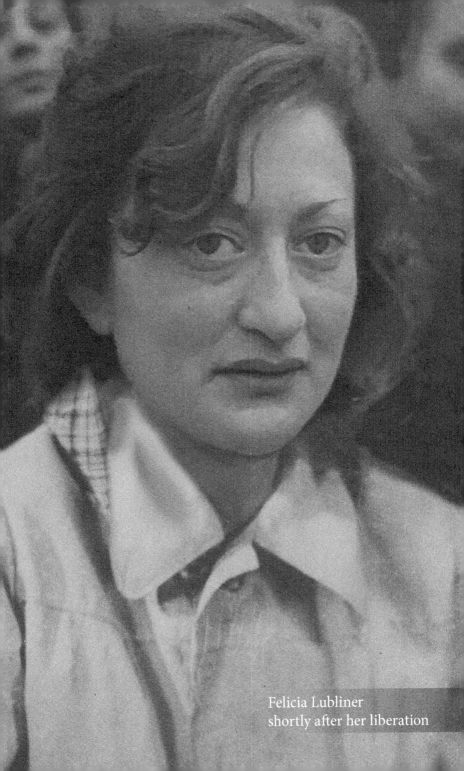

Felicia Lubliner
shortly after her liberation

ONLY HOPE

A SURVIVOR'S STORIES OF THE HOLOCAUST

FELICIA BORNSTEIN LUBLINER

Foreword, afterword,
and edited by Irving Lubliner

[signature] 1-29-25

PUBLISHED BY FELABRA PRESS • ASHLAND, OREGON

Only Hope: A Survivor's Stories of the Holocaust
by Felicia Bornstein Lubliner
© 2019 Irving Lubliner
Published by Felabra Press, Ashland, Oregon
onlyhopebook.com

All rights reserved. No part of this book may be used or reproduced by any means without the written permission of the publisher except in the case of brief quotations embodied in critical articles and reviews.

Book design: booksavvystudio.com

Photo credits:

The photos on pages xiii, xix, 18, 39, 52 are courtesy of Wikimedia Commons; page 27: courtesy Yad Vashem, Wikimedia Commons

Page 31:   courtesy Frankie Fouganthin [CC BY-SA 3.0 (https://creativecommons.org/licenses/by-sa/3.0)

Page 35:   courtesy Oakes, H (Sgt) No 5 Army Film &
            Photographic Unit [public domain]

Page 50:   Bundesarchiv, Bild 101III-Duerr-054-17 / Dürr /
            CC-BY-SA 3.0 [CC BY-SA 3.0 de (https://creativecommons.org/licenses/by-sa/3.0/de/deed.en)]

Page 60:   courtesy of Belarussian State Archive of Documentary
            Film and Photography [public domain]

Page 62: United States Holocaust Memorial Museum
            [public domain]

Page 86: Wikipedia: Bundesarchiv, Bild 183-N0827-318 /
            CC-BY-SA 3.0 licensed under Creative Commons
            Attribution-Share Alike 3.90, Germany

Library of Congress Control Number: 2019903762
ISBN: 978-1-7338847-0-9

First Edition
Printed in the United States of America
5 6 7 8 9 10

*This book is dedicated to
those who perished in the Holocaust.*

Contents

Foreword xiii

Follow Me Into Auschwitz 1

Felicia Lubliner Biographical Timeline 6

A Package of Hope 9

Presentation at San Francisco State
University, 1971 19

Concert at Auschwitz 37

The Legacy 41

Choose Your Weapons 47

The Choice 53

The Reunion 63

Afterword 77

Presentation at San Francisco State
University, 1967 83

Holocaust Oral History Project -
Doris Hobson Letter 110

Glossary 114

Acknowledgements 117

Deportation of Jews from a Polish ghetto, 1943

Foreword

My mother wrote. My father spit. My mother talked. My father spit.

My mother told her stories to anyone who would listen. My father spit.

My mother wanted to share her Holocaust experiences with you, and she did so by writing the stories that you hold in your hand. My father kept his own experiences locked up tight within himself, and then he spit.

Both of them were deeply affected by what they suffered in their teens and twenties. It is baffling to me how they were able to live what those around them—those who didn't know any better—would call "normal" lives. My mother's way of processing and integrating her experiences was to get close to people and then share her deepest secrets, letting them feel her pain. My father kept his pain locked up within, almost until the end of his life.

Shortly after my mother's death, my father was diagnosed with Alzheimer's disease, and I tried caring for him at home. He had always enjoyed stamp collecting, and someone had given him a bag of European stamps from the 30s and 40s. He hardly ever talked at this point, but he was very content to examine and sort the stamps. One night, he was looking over his stamps, one by one, as I graded papers. All of a sudden, he became quite agitated. Looking in his direction, I saw the one in his hand, bearing a picture of Hitler and, if I remember correctly, a swastika. Without saying a word, my father angrily spit on that stamp.

My father did not, as a rule, call attention to himself, and I had never seen him spit. He was also not one to ask others to focus on what he endured and lost as a young adult. He might have fooled those who knew him into thinking that his experiences of the Holocaust were behind him or forgotten. In that moment, however, his spitting left no doubt that his grief and anger had always been there, hidden. Witnessing that, I could tell that his stories were every bit as powerful as my mother's. If only he had chosen or been able to share them.

As I think about my parents' experiences in the Nazi concentration camps, I wonder: *What kept them going? With too little food, death all around them, savage beatings doled out to those not doing their assigned slave labor quickly enough, and the loss of all that had once been dear to them, what could they do to summon the will to live another day?* The only answer that comes to me is: They could hope.

With shattered dreams, interrupted educations, no

homes or family to which they might someday return, and a horrifying day-to-day existence, they could not make plans for their futures. They could only hope.

Would each day's meager food ration provide enough sustenance to stay alive until tomorrow? Would the doctor making the selections of who should live and who should die allow them another day's salvation? If yesterday they were lucky to avoid being singled out by a capricious and malicious guard, would that luck last through another day? They could only hope.

Would the torn rags that had to suffice as clothing provide enough warmth at night to avoid freezing to death? Would the diseases that ran rampant throughout the camps, taking many lives, spare theirs? They could only hope.

My mother, Felicia Lubliner, died in 1974, but she lives on in the pages you are about to read. She also lives on in the hearts and minds of the many people who have read and been impacted by her stories. You are about to enter her world, and I am confident you will be grateful that you decided to go there.

During her teens and early twenties, the Nazis took away all that my mother owned, but they could not take away her dignity. They could not take away her compassion. They could not take away her capacity to love. They could not take away her ability to tell her stories, enabling us to better understand what she, her family members, and so many others endured.

The Nazis tried to take away her will to act on her own behalf. They took away her name and replaced it with a number, tattooed on her arm. They assigned her to slave labor, making it her key to survival. As long as she could work, she could live. She did the seamstress work expected of her, but she also took pleasure in knowing that the coats she was re-making (sewing furs confiscated from incoming prisoners into the linings) for German soldiers being sent to the Russian front had slits cut into them, ensuring that they would fall apart when worn. I am in awe of the brave acts of sabotage she committed.

What the Nazis did not realize was that this determined woman had her own reasons to live. She dreamed of being a wife and mother. She dreamed of surviving the war to share her stories.

When my parents came to the United States in 1949, they knew little or no English. By 1960, my mother had somehow mastered the language and had become a public speaker, published author, and a force to be reckoned with if you were playing *Scrabble*. She had a great laugh and loved to be on stage, making other people laugh. I have fond memories of her volunteer performances at my elementary school Parents' Night talent shows, where she'd do a stand-up comedy routine reminiscent of Zsa Zsa Gabor. She enjoyed and thrived on those performances, using humor to ease her way into a program in which she was the only one speaking with a Polish (or, for that matter, any kind of) accent. As we laughed, she laughed as well. Or at least that's how it seemed.

On the inside, my mother was hurting more than I or anyone else, except perhaps my father (and I'm not even sure about him), could grasp. After her death, I learned that she had been under psychiatric care throughout her adult life for insomnia coupled with recurring nightmares. The sight of a fire in the fireplace, a warm and comforting sight for me, was, for her, a painful reminder of the crematoria in which the bodies of so many people close to her—acquaintances, friends, and family members—were turned to ashes.

Though they came to this country with virtually nothing, my parents somehow managed to purchase a home when I was four years old. My father had held a variety of jobs, sometimes holding down two full-time jobs simultaneously, until he became a warehouse worker with union benefits, at which point one job sufficed. My mother was a seamstress working at home during my early childhood, but she later became a travel agent, specializing in travel to Israel. My father and I were fortunate enough to accompany her on one of her trips to Israel (when I was 14), and I remember that being a cherished time for our family.

I was able to say goodbye to my mother in her final days, as she succumbed to cancer. I was able to say goodbye to my father as his Alzheimer's dementia caused him to wither and detach from my reality. How different it was for my mother to lose her parents. Nazi officers came and took her father away one day, and that was the last the family ever saw of him. She tried to stay with her mother, but they were brutally separated as they stepped off a transport train, never to see each other again. As when her father was taken, there was no opportunity to say goodbye. Sadly, I can't describe what my father went through in losing his parents. I wish I had learned more about his life as a child and young adult, the horrors he endured to survive the war, and the loved ones he lost.

After Mom passed away, I found and gathered these stories, organized them chronologically, and began to share them with school groups and others expressing interest. People's reactions have motivated me to share them more widely. Will these stories find a wider audience and be read even beyond my lifetime? I can only hope.

What follows is the text of a handwritten essay, "Follow Me Into Auschwitz," found among my mother's papers at the time of her death. I do not know how she intended to use it. Perhaps it was to be the introduction to one of her presentations to college students studying the Holocaust. It may have been intended as the beginning of a longer narrative she never had time to write. Whatever its original purpose, I have chosen to let her words serve as a prologue to her stories. Nothing I could write would be as fitting an introduction.

IRVING LUBLINER, 2019

Only Hope

A Survivor's Stories
of the Holocaust

Follow Me Into Auschwitz

MANY BOOKS HAVE BEEN WRITTEN on the subject of the Holocaust, and I am sure that anybody interested enough has had an opportunity to get the facts and figures of the war crimes. There were books describing the Holocaust in great detail, books explaining the events in terms of politics and statistics, and books analyzing the psychological behavior of the victims and their tormenters alike.

There were international tribunals and well publicized trials where the matter was discussed in terms of jurisprudence. There were diaries, novels, movie scripts; in other words, the topic has been almost talked to death.

Yes, there were millions killed, but this astronomical number is meaningless. Those dead have no faces, no voices, no personalities; they are a mass, like grains of sand on a beach. How many Anne Franks have longed and suffered in this multitude? Can anybody find a hint of identification with an emaciated, half-naked, terrorized and tormented creature?

Even as the war was coming to its bitter end, at the time when the Allied armies were pushing toward the heart of Germany, when the *Götterdämmerung* was almost obliterated, when there were not enough trains to transport troops—even then, the death factory at Auschwitz worked around the clock, and the building of barracks was going on.

The Gypsies, Jehovah's Witnesses, and Jews of Europe were, by then, literally wiped out. Millions of others, such as Poles and Russians, had already perished. For whom then were those new barracks built? Several historians, including Constantine Fitzgibbon, who translated the autobiography of Auschwitz commandant Rudolf Höss, have indicated that the concentration camps were indeed intended as a permanent fixture of the Third Reich. Plans had been made to deport every English male over 17 should Great Britain have been occupied by the Nazis.

What would you have done if it were your freedom and your life that were being threatened by the Nazis? What if it were your parents, your children, your brothers and sisters, and your dearest friends that were being taken away, never to be seen again?

Would you have fought the Nazis with your bare hands? Would you have chosen to die by your own hand, rather than let yourself be driven to the gas chambers?

Accusations have been made that Jews behaved cowardly and let themselves be slaughtered by the millions without resistance. This is not true. There was resistance—not only desperate, armed, and heroic, as in the case of the Warsaw Ghetto, but day-by-day resistance and a will to withstand, to outlive.

Death was cheap at Auschwitz. It was ever-present, stinking its way into your very brain, blackening the sky with its smoke, looking at you from the barrels of guns and from the eyes of the condemned. Death was with you during the dreaded roll calls, where at dawn and dusk you stood for endless hours in ankle-deep mud, with only rags between you and the biting chill of the wind.

It was easy to die at Auschwitz; one did not have to be a hero to die. There were many ways you could have saved the SS the work; all you had to do was give up. Give up willingly the spark of life still flickering in you—that last thing you had, which they were so determined to take.

You could have risked your own life and tried to attack an SS guard, as has been suggested by Dr. Bruno Bettelheim in his book, *The Informed Heart*. This, even if it were possible, would have been not only a foolish way to commit suicide, but it would have been murder as well, for, by your so-called heroism, you would have exposed your next of kin, your loved ones, and the rest of your fellow inmates to the uncontrollable fury of SS revenge.

It was easier to just touch the electrified wires crisscrossing the camp site and end it all. The temptation was always there. It was hardest to resist at night. The wires stretched as far as you could see – with the lights strung on them, and the wind playing a weird invitation to death: "Touch me…Come close…Touch me."

It took great strength to resist, but we resisted; I resisted the temptation. Dying makes sense if one has a cause to die for. We had no such cause. We had a great cause to live. By my own death, I could not possibly have saved anybody, nor accomplished anything. It would have been a futile gesture and an easy way out, and it would have proved that deep in my heart I believed that Auschwitz is forever. It would have meant admitting to myself that this screaming, insane world around me represented the universe.

I chose to live. For every hour lived at Auschwitz was a victory, and if I had lost in the end, I would be marching to meet death along with the others without tears, without dramatic outbursts, but in a silence that shrieked its mute protest into the unheeding heavens and a deaf world.

The world was not prepared for Auschwitz. It was, in fact, a place unbelievable even for its inmates. No words can really adequately describe this weird world – unlike anything mankind had ever known. In order to understand its implication, you actually had to be part of it.

I'll have to be autobiographical, but follow me if you will into Auschwitz and spend a day there, and meet some of the people in the nameless mass of bodies. Try, if you will, to feel, even for a moment, that you could have been one of them, that in fact you *were* one of them.

Felicia Lubliner Biographical Timeline

November 1, 1922
Felicia (Felicija) Bornstein is born in Pabianice, Poland to Dora Berlinski (Bertinska?) and Josef (Matis?) Bornstein (Borenstein?). She grew up in a close-knit household that included her parents, her grandmother, and eight siblings.

The children (listed in what is believed to be birth order) were: Celina, Sara, Aram (Moishe?) Luba, Felicia (Fela), Zalman, Guta, Bronia, Esther

Note: Alternate spellings have been found in various documents provided by the United States Holocaust Museum.

November, 1939
The Bornstein family is forced into the Pabianice Ghetto.

May, 1942
The Bornstein family is relocated to the Lodz Ghetto. It is unknown whether the family was still together at this point. Certain family members may have already been deported.

August, 1944
Felicia Bornstein is deported to the concentration camp at Auschwitz.

October, 1944
She is sent to Halbstadt, a sub-camp of the Gross-Rosen concentration camp.

May, 1945
Liberation from the concentration camp and forced labor.

February 1946
Felicia marries Abram Lubliner, also a concentration camp survivor, probably in the Zeilsheim camp for displaced persons.

December 19, 1946
Abram and Felicia's first son, Josef Zvi, is born in Wiesbaden, Germany.

March 7, 1947
Official recording of Abram and Felicia's marriage (in Frankfurt am Main, Germany).

November, 1948
The Lubliner family lives in the Lampertheim camp for displaced persons, created to provide additional space for refugees due to overcrowding at Zeilsheim.

July, 1949
Abram, Felicia, and Josef Lubliner sail to the United States aboard the USS General Eltinge, disembarking in New Orleans. The family resettles in Oakland, California, where they are sponsored as immigrants to the United States by Felicia's aunt, Helen Goldberg.

August 29, 1952
Abram and Felicia's second son, Irving Moshe, is born in Oakland, California.

May, 1961
The San Francisco Chronicle publishes "Concert at Auschwitz" in its Sunday supplement, "This World."

Mid 1950's - 1973
Felicia Lubliner shares her experiences in several public speaking presentations. Among these were multiple appearances in classes studying the Holocaust at San Francisco State University and a segment on the William Winter news and information program on KGO-TV in San Francisco.

April 7, 1974
Felicia Lubliner dies of lung cancer in Oakland, California (at age 51).

A Package of Hope

I CAN BRING THAT DAY BACK ANY TIME, running it like a film in my mind—and the picture never changes. Every figure is as clear and vivid as though the day were yesterday. And, strangely, after so many years, I can still feel the wonderful, incomparable aroma of that day, though so many things have happened since.

There was nothing unusual about the way the day began, and it seemed no different from all the other cold and hungry days of January 1941. The war in Europe was then in its second year, and the Jewish people of Poland were being subjected to persecution that grew steadily worse. The Nazis had taken our homes and belongings and forced us into a ghetto. To earn our skimpy rations of food, we had to work endless hours in the war factories the Germans had set up within the ghetto area. Our meals consisted invariably of thin soup or stewed beets, sometimes a bit of grits, and on rare occasions a few ounces of horsemeat. Though we lived in squalor, hunger, and poverty, we took comfort in the fact that our family—Mother, Father, my six sisters and two brothers—were still together, and somehow life went on.

It was bitterly cold this day. The shimmering, gray frost outdoors emphasized the gray, solid, sad cold inside our tiny, crowded ghetto dwelling. The ice covered the windowpanes, but, by scratching at it with our fingers and melting it with our breath, we made little islands of clear glass so that we could look out at the world beyond.

There was not much to see in the ghetto streets but, if we combined our efforts and cleared a pane in the upper part of the window, by standing on tiptoe we could see a bit beyond the ghetto limits. It was good to see that the ghetto was as white and diamond-studded as the velvety lawns and wide streets of the privileged and free—our dilapidated buildings and broken fences hidden by the thick, white blanket of snow. We could see, too, the proud soldier of the conquering German army—the sentry at the ghetto entrance. Armed and helmeted, he clapped his gloved hands and stamped his heavy boots trying to keep warm.

None of these sights were new or very entertaining, but they helped to pass the time until the big event of the day, the main meal. We did not expect that our menu that day would be different, but it would be hot and, thanks to Mother's genius, even tasty. And we were always hungry—all of us except my little sister. Our

The Bornstein family. Felicia is in the upper right.

nine-year-old lay on a cot in a corner, too weak from malnutrition to do more than smile a little when we tried to amuse her. She was so accustomed to hunger that it was hard to rouse her interest, even at mealtime.

Suddenly there was a loud and official-sounding knock at our door. We stood paralyzed with fear, for in those days a knock at the door meant only calamity. To our relief and surprise, our caller was only a matter-of-fact messenger from the post office. The politeness of his manner was as astonishing as his presence. He announced, quite casually, that a package had arrived for our family from the United States of America and that we could claim it at the militia office across the street. Though the United States was not yet involved in the war with the Nazis, we were dumbfounded, and to this day I cannot understand how the miracle of the package delivery came about. For the Jews of Poland who were not deprived of life itself were deprived of all else but bare subsistence by the conquering German armies.

As I look back at this episode, I think we must have been a ludicrous picture to the young messenger, staring at him, all of us, open-mouthed, as though he were an angel descended from heaven. He beat a hasty retreat, leaving only a slip of yellow paper as our claim document in my mother's hand. As the door closed, we came to life and the commotion soon verged on the hysterical. We embraced, we cried, we laughed, we pinched ourselves and each other, assured ourselves loudly that we were awake, not dreaming, and finally marched triumphantly around my little sister's cot and around the room, again and again, ladles, brushes, and broomsticks clutched in our arms like crusading banners. Mother stood motionless in the midst of the bedlam, a far-away look on her pale, worn face, tears overflowing her dark, beautiful eyes.

When we had calmed down a bit, Father and my two brothers struggled into their shabby jackets, each trying to take permanent hold of the little magic yellow paper. Mother began slowly to regain her powers of speech; half whispering, she began to talk of her sister-in-law, our aunt, who lived in America and of whom she was always so fond. We remembered our aunt from letters and pictures that had arrived regularly before the war, but that seemed ages ago to us. We had been isolated from the world for so long, we had forgotten that somewhere mail is received and sent quite as a matter of course. It seemed inconceivable that anything could have penetrated the thick walls of hatred and discrimination surrounding us.

At the moment, though, we children were not concerned with anything but the package. Back at our watchposts at the window, we each tried to catch first sight of our proudly returning men. When they had arrived and the package was safely deposited on the table, we all stood and simply gazed wordlessly at the package—and in our minds it grew larger and larger and more and more miraculous. I cannot tell you how much that package meant to us, but perhaps you will understand when I say that at that moment we were not even wondering what it contained. It brought us a message—a message of hope, awareness that somewhere there was someone who cared, who loved and remembered. It came as a warm, soft breeze of freedom across an icy sea of cruelty and terror to renew our strength, to remind us to resist, to conquer cold, hunger, fear, and humiliation. All those things the package meant, and more—that package from America.

The spell was finally broken and we watched breathlessly as Father unwrapped the string. Out came cans, boxes and bags, all filled with food, laid on the table with trembling hands. Then the fiesta began.

Mother, always practical and thinking of tomorrow, tried in vain to persuade us to try the goodies one by one. But she soon gave up as we insisted we had to have a taste, at least a taste, of everything—right then and there, that very minute. And so we did.

First, a lick of delicious white powder—it tasted so good. Then out came the sugar, and we tried that and the powder mixed together. It tasted even better. Wait, there were raisins and cocoa, and we thought it would make a wonderful spread for bread to mix it all with the powder. There was laughter when we realized that there was no bread—nothing seemed to depress us at that moment.

Quietly, Mother was taking possession of the rice, canned butter, flour, and other unheard-of luxuries, calculating in her mind how many days she could stretch the treasures to enrich our meager meals. And then out of the package came the meat. It was brown, looked like any ordinary smoked meat, but there was something magical about it. I know now it was the heavenly smell that issued from it.

Mother took it to the stove, after we had made her promise to cook all of it right away. We unanimously voted in favor of having one good dinner, rather than have our meals strengthened for a few days, as Mother and reason would have dictated.

Having gained this overwhelming victory, we settled comfortably to wait for the big meal of the day. We sat hugging the hot stove, nibbling and munching, studying the labels in foreign languages on the cans and boxes, and after a while we deciphered them all. But by the time we figured out that the white powder was nothing but powdered milk, we had almost eaten it all up by spoonfuls. It tasted good, too, even though it had a disturbing tendency to form a hard paste in our mouths.

It was an idle, contented waiting. We watched Mother, who, like a high priestess bending over the fire, performed the rituals of her divine cooking. The intoxicating, heavenly fragrance of the meat filled the room like incense from an altar.

Meanwhile, the news of the Package had spread like wildfire over the ghetto, along with that aroma seeping out from our doors and windows. We were a family of eleven and we each had our friends, but until that afternoon we never realized how frighteningly many we had.

All of a sudden, all of these friends seemed to feel duty-bound to pay us a visit, and soon we witnessed a procession of people with such a genuine concern about our well-being that we were touched. They came in a steady flow, with all kinds of excuses, and problems to be talked over without delay; they asked advice, they gave us advice, but very few of them admitted having ever heard about the package.

They all, however, commented on the wonderful smell, and there was even a clever one who brazenly asked Mother for the recipe to bring this smell out in horsemeat.

Mother didn't seem to mind all of this; rather she seemed to enjoy it thoroughly. To each and every one of these visitors, she proudly told the story of her favorite sister-in-law in America, how she always knew we were not forgotten by the free world outside, and how she had never lost faith in God.

The guests nodded and marveled, their eyes darting toward the food, but none of them would leave without having tasted a bit of that famous meat. We watched fearfully, afraid there wouldn't be anything left for us. Mother always loved to entertain generously, and there was no stopping her now, even if she chose to give away the last morsel.

She very nearly did, for when we finally sat down to that long-awaited meal, our portions had shrunk to almost microscopic size. There wasn't enough of it to get the flavor—but that is not important, for the wonderful fragrance of the meat crept forever into our memories. It is still in mine, staying with me all these years, along with all the little details which made that day unforgettable…the day the Package of Hope arrived.

Editor's Note:

What follows is a transcript of a presentation my mother gave in Professor Irving Halperin's course on the Holocaust at San Francisco State University on April 20, 1971.

Whereas the other stories were crafted and probably resulted from several typewritten drafts, here my mother is unedited, sharing her thoughts aloud before a live audience.

∽

Presentation at San Francisco State University, 1971

[Editor's note: It is possible that a few minutes of the presentation went unrecorded and were lost.]

Well, then there is hunger, which a lot of people—and I was guilty of that too—I never knew what hunger is. I always used to come home, said, "Mom, I'm hungry. I'm starved."

Well, hunger, you don't feel it in here, you feel it in your brain because a constant hunger is something else than just an appetite. And a lot of people do confuse it. Hunger is knowing that you're not going to have anything to eat tomorrow, or a day after, or a day after. And then it eats into your brain and you know it, and you just can't sleep because you think of food. How you're going to get it? Are you going to have it?

Well, but somehow you eat leaves and all kinds of things that are edible, coffee grinds or such grinds, whatever you can find. And you hope that this is all, that this is going to end, and the war is going to be over one day. You have to believe that the war is going to be over.

And then one day there is an order that comes very rationally presented by the German authorities that the front is coming nearer and we need the Jewish people for our war effort. They have to—because we did work in the ghettos; everybody had to in order to get the ration, scanty as it was—but we need the people to help us out in another area. Therefore, we are going to resettle. And people should volunteer for resettlement.

Well, a lot of people—and this is a strange thing how they had everybody fooled, that a lot of people had considering volunteering for resettlement. But common sense prevailed most cases because, in the course of events, after living two or three years in different ghettos and having gone through so much already, you know that you cannot trust Nazis. So you keep from volunteering, but you think, "Well, what can be worse? After all, we are starving here." Disease is going to get you one way or another. But then, "No, if they want us, let them come and get us."

And come and get us they did. And now, if any of you have seen the picture of Anne Frank, the film, and if you remember the last scene, when they broke into the house and everybody was speechless. And that's what it was like, because you're paralyzed. You look at the barrel of a gun and look into it, and there's death looking at you from it. You can't say anything, so you pick up your bundle and go. We did take bundles because we thought, well, for resettlement they told us to take along all our valuables—clothing, utensils, everything—just like a normal moving thing.

So now, if you follow me, we'll go together to the station, to the collecting station, and there you are being counted. The train drives up to the siding, and you are marched up to the train. It's a cattle train, and the doors are being locked from the outside and bolted, and the guards are mounting the platforms. And you are suddenly in a different world, in a train that's beginning to move, but has no windows, and it's full of people.

And so you're surrounded by bodies, and you jostle against each other, and you fight for breath. And before you boarded the train, you were given a little loaf of bread, which kind of lulls your senses because you feel, "Well, if you were going to death, why the hell would they give you bread?" So you clutch that little piece of bread, and you don't know that it will have to last you for three days or whatever it will take them to get you to your destination, and the destination is unknown.

And there's a lot of speculation in the train, going out. As it moves through the countryside, and people are climbing on each other's shoulders to try to peek out and see where we're going—or where you're going, because you're with me now. And nobody can tell, but there's a lot of speculation and people—there's always an optimist that would say, "Well, they're going to put us to work. We've worked before and maybe we'll work another few months and the whole thing will be over, and we'll go back and start a normal life again."

And there was always a pessimist who said, "No, they're going to kill us all." Nobody wanted to believe that. How can anyone think anything that monstrous? And why would anybody want to kill us? That was the question.

So the train glides and rolls through the night, and you have to fight for your breath, you have to fight for space. There's no place to lie down, so you stand up. People that died overnight kind of are held up with the others, so there's a bit of room made in the corner for them.

And finally you arrive at the destination, and this is the end of the line. And the train—it's early afternoon and the doors of the train open, and you step out into a different world. It's unbelievable to you because there's nothing to keep your mind on, to hang it on. No peg, nothing in the past that would connect with any scene like this.

At first, there is a reception committee. They tell you to step off, and there is a voice from a loudspeaker telling you that you've come to your destination, and this is a camp where you're going to work. And on the gate—there is a gate, an iron gate, and on the gate there is a legend which says, *Arbeit macht frei*, which translated into English means, "Work sets you free." And it isn't till much later, after you've been there for a while, that you realize that the inscription should have said, "Abandon all hope, ye who enter here."

Well, you come down, and there's a reception committee consisting of guards with guns and bayonets, big German Shepherds and Doberman dogs. You're surrounded. From the distance there is a band playing and that makes it even more weird. You see a lot of wires, wire fences about six foot high, crisscrossing in every direction. And you're told to step out, and you're told to leave all your belongings there; they will be delivered to you later. And you're also told that the older people and the children will have to go to a different part of the camp where they will be taken care of. And the young people will go to a work camp.

So you separate from your mother and your father, and you look at her and she's trying to tell you something, and you don't quite know whether to leave her or not, but then you're pushed by the others, and everything is—the orders come then in such rapid succession, and everything is quick, quick, that you don't have time to think. So you leave with the others, the young people.

Then there is another order that men should go separately—that's from the young group—and the women go separately. So there's another separation. You separate from your brothers, if one has a husband or lover, and then you are again alone with women only.

And you'll be marched down a street which looks like no street in the world. It consists of wire fences on each side of you, and beyond those fences you see barracks, buildings, clustered one next to the other, very orderly, in all a line on each side.

There's some strange-looking people standing in front of the barracks. Some of them wear pajama-like outfits, striped, and they yell at you, and they said, "Oh, you're new here, you'll have to adjust." So you feel you'll have to adjust. And it's so unreal because you really don't feel you'll have to adjust because this is not … not happening.

And then you walk a little farther and you look through the wire, and there is a field and a lot of people running around there. But they don't look like people; they look like scarecrows, like some weird insane creatures. Their heads are shaven, they wear rags, and they yell at you. And you don't understand what they're trying to tell you. And they can't get close to you because that fence is electrified, so they stand at a distance and they keep shouting. And you try to make out.

In the meantime, they're pushing you from behind, the orders come to move fast, the band is playing somewhere in the distance; you don't know what's going on. And the trains come in and unload more people. You just don't realize what's going on, and it's kind of a weird, insane thing, and it's like a nightmare.

And then you finally make out what these people are shouting at you. And yes, by close look you discover that these naked skulls and these shaven people, they are women. You finally make out what they're shouting at you. They shout to you to throw that little piece of bread that you might have left from the train journey. They shout, "Throw it to us because they will take it away." But you don't believe them because these people are insane, apparently, and that is why they look like this, and that's why they are kept behind fences. That's how you reason, because there is no other explanation that you know for this kind of a world.

And you come a little farther, and you come to a barracks, and there you are told to strip. Nowadays it's kind of a common thing to see people strip, even in the street, and nobody gives it a second thought. In those days, to have—and that's a voluntary stripping, that's different, but if you are told to strip, it's a different story. You're ordered to. And you still clutch photographs and pictures and things that you think you might keep. And leave everything here and you're driven into a shower-type thing.

And in the meantime, you are thinking, what happened to your mother? Is she going into the same type of shower? Is she with other people with somebody taking care of her? What's happening to her? But then you feel, "Well, she probably is with older people and they will take care of her."

You go through that shower, ice-cold. You come out on the other side, and there is a barber. He shaves your hair. He shaves your body hair. And you feel—I don't know whether you would know this: it's an awful thing for a girl to have a shaven hair. We looked at each other at first, but you couldn't see yourself. So you see the others and it looks so terribly, hysterically funny that you cry yourself laughing. But then you don't know that you look just the same to others. And all of this is happening so fast, you really haven't got time to think what is really happening or what place this really is.

Well, you are brought to a barracks again, one of those buildings that you saw passing by, and it's a long, narrow structure with nothing in it. They were like stall-like, all the compartments on each side. And the naked, mud-packed floor. You're told to sit down in rows of five. I guess they used five because it was easier for them to count us that way. So you sit in a row of five, straddling the person next to you, between your legs, and the person next to you between the other's legs, and so you sit. And that's how you're going to sit for days, and that's how you're going to sleep, in a row of five, and if one has to turn, so all four have to turn. If you're lucky you might get an old horse blanket for five, which, if you get a corner

of it in a chilly night, that's pretty good.

They feed you in fives. You're given an old rusty pot with some watery, sandy soup in it, and you're told, "This is for five of you." No spoon. How do you divide it, do you think? Well, we devised a system whereby you counted the swallows. You took five full swallows of the soup and passed it to the next one in back of you. She did. And then while you did it, while you had your five swallows you were watched by eight hungry eyes. Four other hungry people watched you, that you don't cheat, that you don't have six swallows of soup. And you, in turn, watch the others because you are just as hungry. And that was going on.

Now, that was a time—there were a lot of people that were brought—that was Auschwitz. We didn't know even the name when we first came there—you don't know it, but you find out later on.

And you look out and there are two—you see two big chimneys against the sky, tall chimneys, with smoke and fire belching out of it day and night. And you begin to wonder what is being burned there. After all, you've been told that you're going to work, so perhaps this is a factory. Well then, if it's a factory, who's working there, and why don't they put us to work, finally?

They did put some people to work, and some people were just sitting there to wait, either to be—well, let's not jump ahead—we'll wait for we don't know what.

And somebody suggested that in this fire that you see burning, is because they burn our hair there. They burn your papers, your photographs, anything. But they don't burn your mother there. And you know that they do, but you don't want to believe it. You can't believe it because if you do, then you go insane! So you try to fool yourself that it's not so. Didn't quite succeed, but you're so busy trying to survive—and again, why survive because you feel, what's the use? You survive and you get sent up there anyway, or it's not going to end well anyway.

Many things have been said about people going to death like sheep, not putting up resistance. Well, there was thought of resistance, and there was resistance. We had passive resistance long before this word became fashionable on campuses.

The resistance was to just stay alive, to just keep human. Because if you committed suicide or if you gave up faith in life, then it was admitting to yourself that Auschwitz is forever. It was admitting to yourself that this insane world is part of you and you're part of it, and that's how it should be. And you gave up.

But death was very cheap at Auschwitz. It was so easy to die; it took no heroism. Death looked at you from the barrels of the guns. It looked at you from the eyes of the examining doctor. It looked at you from the eyes of the people going to these, toward those chimneys, in big vans. It was everywhere; it stunk its way into your brain. But you couldn't accept that; otherwise, you just can't function. And every hour lived at Auschwitz was a victory.

You could have touched the wire, the electrically charged wire, and you would be put out of misery in a moment. And then you would be lined up with the morning count or the evening count, along with the others. You wouldn't stand; you would be lined up. They lined the dead up, too. Because you're counted twice a day. Because so many people have to feed—have to go to the crematorium or to the gas chamber. It contained two thousand at a time, and so there was a quota, a daily quota, that the Nazis had to fill.

And so they made selections. They had to have their people—nobody could escape. Not a mouse could escape from this place probably, but they still—the counting was twice a day, once at dawn, and once in the evening, where they lined you up in rows of five again, and you stood there for hours waiting to be counted. And if one person in your whole block—the blocks were, a barracks was called a block—had misbehaved or had stolen a potato peel or went out of line in some other way—there were millions of ways to go out of line—one person, then everybody in the camp had to stand as a punishment for hours till you dropped. And that went on day after day, twice a day.

And then there were the selections. Now, the

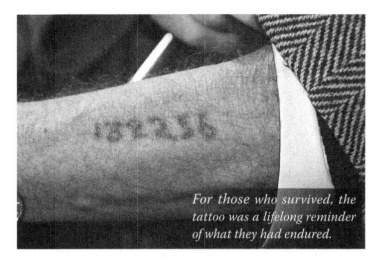

For those who survived, the tattoo was a lifelong reminder of what they had endured.

selections were a device to find people to either go to work outside, because different factories within Germany had sent their representative to pick people capable to work for slave labor. On the other hand, those people that had lost enough weight, developed some pimples, or looked sick enough, they were no longer useful, and they were sent to the gas chambers immediately. So there were selections.

And it was done by a doctor, so-called doctor. Impeccably dressed in his uniform, white gloved, and you passed in front of him, stripped, and he looked you over. And he, with a nod of his head or a motion of his hand, decided whether you were going to live or die.

Recht to links, right or left. One group formed to the right; one group formed to the left. You never knew what group was going where. The system that they had was so foolproof, because, even if you tried to escape from one group to another, you really never knew which one is going out of the camp to some factory to really work, and which one is going to the gas chambers.

So you try your best to look good. How do you look good when you have skin and bones only? You're pale, so you rub brick dust on your cheeks to give color. That's the rouge of Auschwitz. And, if you're lucky, you pass the inspection and you live another few days, and perhaps another few days, and so it goes. But day by day, and every day that you live, you feel you've lived an eternity. But you did not make it any easier for them by letting them take you.

So, you have no privacy. You're surrounded by bodies, unwashed, because if you wanted to wash you had to do it at the risk of your own life. You….you're just dehumanized. The process of dehumanization goes on because you're conditioned to obey orders only, and not to think. And the only way to preserve a spark of humanity is to think. And this is what you do.

The nights when you cannot sleep, you get acquainted with people next to you, and you find out that underneath this parchment-like skin and under this bare rib cage, there is a heart that is warm, and a brain that works, and you find a kinship sometimes with someone. I'd like to meet you some of the people in your block…I'd like you to meet some of the people on the block.

There is a sculptress. I'll never forget her, and I hope you won't. Pale, thin, she was thrown a rag—we all were thrown rags right in the beginning which we had to—you had to—keep all the way through. And it consisted of some very incongruous looking things, like a blouse that's too long or too short, a garment with one sleeve or no sleeves at all, no underwear at all, no shoes. It was cold out there in the morning and in the evening, and the area where this camp is located is, because of the rains that would begin to fall, turned into absolute mire-like, swamp-like area. So you sink your ankles in that mud, but you learned to even walk through that.

And you learned to—you share with each other. You share the books that you read before, poems that you knew, ideas that you had, you shared them with others, and others shared them with you. That is how you remained at least human a little bit, at certain times, in spite of the fact that you respond like an animal to everything, to your body's demands for food, for other things.

And this girl, the sculptress, we named her "Butterfly" because her rag was very colorful, and it looked incongruous in those bleak surroundings. She looked like a very exotic butterfly with this big, too-big dress on her skinny body. You were given a little piece of bread a day, and again it was a tiny little loaf to be divided by five. This and the soup was your sustenance for the day. And how you divide a little loaf of bread by five is by taking off a piece of your rag that you wear and measuring it, and then tearing off pieces so nobody will get cheated.

Well, she managed to save, Butterfly managed to save, a little crumb every day of that bread. And she used it. She was making little figurines out of it. And she decorated it with little threads that she found, or grains of sand. And they were the most exquisite pieces of art made out of little rolled-up bread crumbs. She was still clutching one of those figurines in her hand when she was taken away during one selection, and never seen again. She went to the other side.

There is next to you, perhaps, someone—these people that I remember most—a lady doctor who studied in Kiev before the war, and she got a group of people together and taught them Russian. There was a dress designer who painted or made drawings of dresses in the sand, to keep doing things, to keep her mind occupied. There was no, of course, no paper, no nothing, you just—well, the Nazis pretty nearly succeeded in bringing human beings to the level of animals. Pretty nearly.

But there was that inner strength that you tried to preserve, and you do tell yourself, you do tell yourself over and over again, that it's they who are the animals, and you are human. And there is that constant fight to preserve every bit of human feeling and not let them bring you down to this level. And when you're beaten—and you are beaten, and kicked—you still think that it's he that's

Female camp guards

the animal. And you wouldn't, probably, want to trade places with him. You somehow do feel superior, even as a victim. You can if you have enough of inner strength.

[Editor's note: A few seconds were lost at this point as the first recorded tape was replaced with the second.]

...all these difficulties. And the nightmare goes on. And yet—I'm trying to find the right words for you to feel like—you know you're going to wake up, and so you struggle to, when you do wake up, to at least be human. And if you lose in the end, you would go to your death, along with the others, and in spite whatever else you might have read in certain books, the people did die with dignity.

They died, and you would go with them quietly, without tears, but in a silence that—a shrieking silence—could there be such a thing as a shrieking silence? That's what it was. You wonder how long this is going to take and no word reaches you from the outside. You know that there is a world outside somewhere, if you could only reach it.

And you stored things in your memory, and you'd say to each other, "Let's not ever forget any of it. Because if we do come out alive with this, if we do wake up from this insane nightmare, we have to bring the message to make sure that this thing will never happen again."

Concert at Auschwitz

I WAS SENT TO AUSCHWITZ late in 1944 when the war in Europe was already five years old. For us, the Jewish people in Poland, those were long, terror-filled years when I learned the paralyzing effect of fear—when my healthy young appetite was replaced by hunger that kept me awake at night, gnawing inside like a worm, and when the only defense against humiliation was our contempt for the tormenters.

I was already then a veteran of two ghettos and had lost trace of my father and two sisters who were sent away and never heard from again. I thought I had seen and lived through the worst. Then I came to Auschwitz. I remember every day and everything that occurred, but some things—fragments and pictures—stand out more sharply in focus.

One of them is this unbelievable picture of my first day in Auschwitz. There I was, dressed in pitiful rags thrown to me at random after my clothes had been taken away, barefoot, with no undergarments. My freshly shaven head was naked and shamefully exposed. I was sobbing in despair.

I was separated from my mother when we came off the train. I did not know then what was happening to her—that she was being led to the gas chambers to die. I longed to be with her—she looked so forlorn and frightened as we were forced apart.

"Cry, cry, little one," whispered someone in my ear. "It is good for you. I, too, cried when I first came here. We all did, but we have no more tears left. Look around and see for yourself."

I raised my head and looked at what seemed to be only a blur of faces and a multitude of people surrounding me, all packed so close together there was no room to move about. It was quiet except for an occasional moan, sigh, cough or whisper.

"How long have you been here?" I asked my new friend.

"I don't know exactly," she answered. "It has been such a long time—maybe a month—we lose all track of time here. We just wait."

"Wait for what?" I asked.

"Wait to be free—we will be free some day—we must believe this," she said, "or else…"

She did not finish her sentence, for suddenly a large door was thrown wide open and a burst of bright daylight

SS. Officer Irma Grese

almost blinded me. There was considerable commotion and orders shouted. My heart stood still with fear. When I dared to look up again, a few women were standing in the doorway, listening attentively to orders being given by the head of the group.

This leader was a young woman in an SS uniform with a culotte skirt and riding boots. In one of her white-gloved hands, she carried a riding crop; the other rested on her hip, where she wore a holster and pistol.

My friend whispered to me: "She is Irma Grese. We call her the 'Angel of Death.' Don't move now—don't let her notice you or single you out."

As it turned out this particular morning, Irma Grese was in a mood to be entertained and wanted music. She had heard that among this group was a former star of the Warsaw Opera and wanted to hear her sing.

A young woman was ordered out of the crowd of inmates. She still showed traces of beauty on her emaciated face, in spite of her shaven head. Her naked body could be seen through the holes of her tattered garment.

As she began to sing, Irma Grese stood quietly, listening to the beautiful arias, *Lieder*, and folksongs which poured forth in an uninterrupted stream.

The young woman sang of love, beauty, and peaceful nature, while outside the smokestacks of the crematoria billowed clouds of fire and smoke which covered the sky for miles.

When I looked about me, I saw the effect of the beautiful music on my fellow inmates—they were motionless, but tears were streaming down their faces. I was amazed to see that they did have tears left—the memories of long-forgotten days of happiness breaking through the despair of hopelessness.

There was no applause.

After the concert ended, Irma Grese walked away quietly. On the way back to her quarters, she calmly shot a girl for raiding the garbage can in search of potato peelings.

The Legacy

BLOCK 31 IN COMPOUND C, AUSCHWITZ CAMP for Women, was a long rectangular barracks, windowless (like all the others) except for small slits high up near the ceiling. Only when the heavy doors were open did sunlight enter the gloom of the narrow interior. Compound C was divided from the rest of the camp by an eight-foot wire fence charged with high-voltage electricity. A sign on the barracks door read: THE BLOCK IS YOUR HOME—KEEP IT CLEAN; inside, heavily guarded, and crowded together in unbelievable squalor, over a thousand women awaited their fate.

I do not recall how long I had been in Auschwitz when Lily and her sister, who came to be called "Butterfly," arrived in our compound, but even after seventeen years, I recall them vividly. What happened to Lily and Butterfly was typical of the nightmarish existence in the concentration camp, but seeing the incident as I did imprinted it in my memory forever.

Ours was a transit barracks and its occupants were changed frequently. Some were sent to labor camps, but the majority were taken off to feed the crematoria. Only Dr. Mengele, who made the "selections," decided the inmates' fates. With a wave of his hand or a nod of his head, he had already sent thousands to their death.

Those of us in Block 31 waited, clinging to desperate hope. We did not doubt for a moment that the Nazis would lose the war, but as day after day went by and our bodies grew thinner and weaker, so did our hopes of living to see their defeat.

In the interim between selections we followed a rigid routine. Though no work was assigned to us, we had at all times to keep order. In endless rows of five, we sat on the mud floor. In rows of five, we slept on that same floor, our bodies overlapping, a tangled mess of arms, legs, and shaven heads, shivering in the cold of the night.

Once a day, a watery soup was distributed in the barracks. The five scant portions were measured into a battered container and it was up to the women to share it equally among themselves. Every bit of the food was precious and, as there were no spoons, we drank the hot liquid right from the pot—five gulps each. Then to the next—five gulps—and "pass it on." Each swallow was watched intently by four pairs of hungry, anxious eyes.

By rows of five we were counted at dawn, and again at sundown. For what seemed endless hours, we were compelled to stand in the mud, or kneel with hands raised, waiting for the officers to complete their count. Hundreds died each day, from malnutrition, dysentery, or beatings, and these, too, were placed in rows of five. And the victims of executions and the suicides also—neatly sorted in lines of five.

After the evening count, the highlight of the day was a small piece of bread, which was to last to the next evening. Hunger was so constant it dominated mind and body—even the fear of imminent death did not stop our thought of food. Only when we spoke of the past could we sometimes forget, for a moment, the gnawing pangs.

Lily and Butterfly silently complied with all the rules, always together. They sat beside each other, tried to keep each other warm at night, and shared even the one pair of shoes they had somehow managed to keep.

Talking with Lily and her sister during those long, almost unreal days of horror, I learned that they were the only survivors of what had once been a large, close-knit, happy family. Their parents, sisters, and brother all had been taken away during various selections, and the girls did not know what had happened to them. The two had promised each other they would not be separated, and if they had to die, they would die together. They feared to be apart even for a moment, lest the separation become permanent. We called Lily's sister "Butterfly" because the tattered dress she wore was printed with butterflies, an incongruous, quite ridiculous note of life and color in our bleak surroundings. At night, I could hear them whispering to one another, recalling their family and home and the happy days they had once known.

Schnell, schnell, schnell, the dreaded call came one morning, just as soup was being distributed. Outside, Dr. Mengele and his committee were waiting. The guards, with dogs straining at their leashes, surrounded the compound. The shouted orders came amidst the clamor of the dogs: "Hurry! Out of the barracks! *Alles raus!*" Everything happened so fast, there was not time to hesitate, to think. Obediently, we ran out into the ankle-deep mud. We were ordered to strip and to goose-step before Dr. Mengele—the selection was on. In the distance, a band played *Ach du Lieber Augustin.*

In the confusion, everyone tried to get to the end of the line. Those in the rear rubbed brick-dust into their cheeks—perhaps if they looked healthy they would be chosen for work. But Dr. Mengele did not look at faces—a few ounces of flesh on the body were what made the difference between life and death.

Outside the fence the long rows of trucks could be seen, waiting for the "chimney" selection. In my fear, I did not look at the doctor, but I could hear him humming to the tune of the band. "To the right," he ordered, and I found myself reprieved. I had been chosen for the work brigade—while on my left, skeleton-like figures formed an increasing group. It was then that I looked for Lily and her sister, for they had been right behind me in the line. For a terrifying second, I held my breath. Only when they, too, were ordered to the right, did I seem to breathe again. Butterfly and her sister were still together. The ordeal seemed to be over for us, at least for this day.

It began suddenly to rain heavily and Dr. Mengele hurried to leave. The trucks were beginning to move as the victims were ordered to climb into them. As the doctor walked to his waiting car, he passed near our group, where Lily and Butterfly still stood, holding each other's hands. He must have noticed their close resemblance for he pointed a finger at them, asking, "Sisters?" They nodded. He grinned at first, then pointing to Butterfly, shouted, *RAUS!* Butterfly moved forward, but Lily, too, stepped out of the ranks, still holding her sister's hand.

In the next second, the guards had pulled the clinging girls apart and were dragging Butterfly to the trucks. Lily ran after her but a kick from a guard sent her sprawling in the mud. His boot held her there while, head raised, her face covered with mud, she screamed and begged to be allowed to go with her sister. "Please, please, let me go, too. I want to die with her—together, please, please."

I saw Butterfly clamber into the truck, hesitating only long enough to tear from her feet the shoes she had worn that day, tossing them toward Lily. They made a "plopping" sound as they fell into the mud near her. I could not see Butterfly's face, but I remember the closely-packed bodies of the emaciated women and the hundreds of haunting eyes that looked back from the rapidly moving truck. And in the mud, the sobbing, prostrate body of Lily, her arms reaching out for the shoes.

Choose Your Weapons

L ITTLE WAS KNOWN ABOUT DAVID AND OTTO or their lives in the past, but one could tell just by looking at them that they were worlds apart. They probably would never have met in an ordinary lifetime. However, this was 1944, and they were both prisoners of war in a concentration camp, thrown together by the chaos of war in Europe.

There were about 500 inmates in this compound, giving their last bit of strength to their enemies—forced to work toward German victory. The ages of the inmates ranged from 18 to 45, but they all looked very much alike in their striped uniforms. Five long, agonizing years of war and suffering had stamped them with a certain similarity. They were a pitiful and emaciated lot, but David was the most emaciated of them all. His body was so thin one could see his bones sticking out through his rags. With parchment-colored skin drawn tightly over his gaunt face, he looked like a corpse. His ageless face betrayed no emotion—only his eyes, large, dark and glowing, displayed his determination to live.

With an unyielding doggedness, David shuffled to work every day and did his backbreaking job in the quarry for endless hours, along with his fellow prisoners. Back in the compound, he patiently stood in line for his meager daily ration of food and then shuffled to his cot where he went to sleep as soon as he had demolished the last crumb. He never smiled, seldom spoke to anyone, and had no friends and seemingly no interest in acquiring them. He stayed out of quarrels and disputes and, above all, avoided contact with Otto.

Otto was a *kapo* (trustee), who had worked his way up to this dubious position by informing on others, by the strength of his muscle, his ruthlessness and cruelty. He was trying hard to please his masters, and they liked the way he ran things for them. They could hardly have done a better job themselves! The SS guards could depend on Otto to be an efficient camp leader, for he had quickly learned their methods of treating inmates and applied them with zest and vigor, in fact, adding a gleeful touch of his own.

Otto was rewarded for his efforts. Well-fed and dressed, exempt from work, he had an abundance of energy to use on his fellow inmates who learned to fear him as much as his SS pals. David had seen Otto's type before in other camps; he tried to make himself inconspicuous; he avoided being singled out from the crowd. However, he realized after a time that Otto, who was in charge of distribution of food, was robbing the inmates of their scant portions. While every ounce of bread meant a difference of life or death for the prisoners, Otto was trading their rations to keep himself supplied with cigarettes and liquor. David realized that he and his fellow sufferers would be kept alive only as long as their strength permitted them to work. He knew the gas chambers and crematoria were waiting for those who could not go on. And David was determined to go on. He desired to live, if only to see the Nazis defeated.

With anger and desperation bolstering his courage, he went to the SS Colonel in charge of the camp. The officer did not like the idea of inmates standing up for their rights. He expected them to take their treatment as a matter of course, which, out of fear, they usually did. The Colonel placed the matter in Otto's hands, and Otto was only too eager to do the dirty work. From then on, David's fate was sealed and his life made so miserable that everyone wondered how he had the strength to stand it all.

Otto made David his pet project, beating him regularly every day until his body was one gaping sore. His teeth were kicked out and his face swollen beyond recognition. Otto was out to teach David a lesson, and he did it with a thoroughness and system worthy of a Gestapo member in good standing. David became an outstanding example of what happens when one dares to complain.

A Kapo

In addition, he was ordered to bring coffee from the kitchen every day, a most dreaded ordeal and a task that the inmates had ordinarily shared in turn. Now, it was David's job to be awakened brutally every night and to cross the compound shivering in his rags, only to have to run all the way back carrying the huge kettles with the burning liquid spilling and scalding his body. Before going to work, the inmates were given a little "ersatz" which looked and tasted like dishwater, but Otto enjoyed good coffee, which was brought to him in a separate container.

David went to the kitchen every night without complaint. He took his daily beating without a murmur. He dragged his sore body to work along with the others and, to everyone's amazement, he lived on. In spite of Otto's cruelty, David hung on to his life with a strange obstinacy. He talked even less than before, but his eyes had lately acquired a puzzling expression, like a spark of laughter. Everyone thought he had lost his mind and there seemed to be no hope for him. This gruesome contest went on as long as Otto enjoyed it, but as day after day went by, it became monotonous even to him. Otto lost interest in the game, and to save his face, he found a way to stop it. One day the impossible happened. In a sudden and unexpected fit of generosity, Otto announced that David had had enough punishment and would now be restored to the normal life of the camp.

At first, David did not seem to understand and he stood speechless. When he regained his composure, he asked, "Is it true? Do you really mean it?"

Otto seemed proud of himself, replying, "Yes, I mean it. I shall leave you in peace from now on."

"In that case," David said, a toothless grin on his face, "from now on, I'll stop pissing in your coffee."

Polish Jews soon after their liberation

The Choice

I COULD HEAR THE CLAMORING NOISE long before I saw the crowd appear on the village road. Shouts, jeers, laughter, and lively sounds of accordion music reverberated in the clear morning air. An odd procession made its way toward the camp, and as they came nearer I began to recognize familiar shapes and faces. There was Andre in the lead, with a broad grin on his face, playing his ever-present accordion, and right behind him a group of men surrounding a lone female figure marched somberly and grimly, and all about them a multitude of grotesque-looking women—my fellow inmates. With their eyes shining and big in their thin faces, their shaven, naked skulls, and bony limbs protruding from the ill-fitting rags, they looked like giant, swarming insects.

The crowd grew larger and larger as more women came out of the barracks, joined the group and merged with it. It seemed as if they were sucked into a growing, wriggling body with a common emotion on its countless faces, and common scorn in its raised fists. A mob.

The chorus of voices rose into deafening din as the crowd approached the barracks door where I stood watching and waiting. It was then that I saw the captive in their midst.

I looked at Mathilde again and again as if to make sure that my eyes were not deceiving me. It was almost impossible to imagine that this creature before me was the same Mathilde I had known for many months, Frau Obersturmführerin Mathilde Bauer in command of the camp. We called her the Monster, and how well she deserved that name! How well she had used her power to make our lives a miserable existence, and how proud she seemed to be of her position. Her power and pride were gone now. They had disappeared overnight, as did the emblems and swastikas from the village buildings, where now white flags of surrender were fluttering in the breeze.

Everything was different this beautiful spring morning, and it was a transformed Mathilde I saw before me. Instead of the despised green uniform with the insignia of terror, she now wore a shabby housedress; a pair of worn slippers replaced the shiny black boots; her cherished peroxide-blonde locks were shorn off her head, revealing black hair roots and ridiculously big ears. I should have liked to watch her face when the cold metal of the clippers had touched her scalp. Had she felt as I did when it was done to me?

The new Mathilde looked almost like one of us, her former victims. Almost—but for her well fed, plump body and chubby cheeks, which were still in sharp contrast with our skeleton-like figures. But it was she who was afraid now. Fear contorted her thin mouth and rounded her watery blue eyes. She was whining and begging for mercy, the Monster whom I had known to shout orders, threats, and insults in a voice filled with contempt and hatred. "I just followed orders," she kept whimpering, but only a few days ago she had had us whipped for not having worked fast enough. She had given the orders to the guards and had stood there grinning, counting the strokes. She had known we were weakened by hunger. She had known it well, for it was she who had withheld our food for days for no reason at all. And how she had enjoyed her fine meals while she forced us to look on, with nothing to swallow but our saliva.

And only last night, just a few hours ago, before they fled in the dark, she and her faithful guards made sure that we would be blown up in the giant fireworks, all six hundred of us, defenseless, starving women to be sacrificed in a final gesture of loyalty to their fallen gods. They would have succeeded had it not been for Pierre and his friends—our friends. These were the French prisoners from a nearby camp with whom we had worked side by side. We were never allowed to speak to them, but we had known them to be friends, even if only by their encouraging smiles. And last night it was Pierre who first came with the wonderful news of freedom. He didn't just come in; he burst into our barracks with triumph on his face and a heavy sack on his shoulders, a giant Atlas with a hundred pounds of sugar on his back.

Spellbound, we watched him as he placed his burden in the middle of the barracks, and then stepped aside with a gallant bow, saying, *Voila! Vive la liberté!* We gathered around and dipped our hands into the contents of the sack, tasting the sweet, sparkling sugar. We ate it by the handful, licking our fingers and smacking our lips, trying to saturate ourselves with its sweetness and that first exhilarating hour of freedom.

Then the others came, all the people from the French barracks, the Italian, the Greek, the men and the women, and for the first time we talked to each other and shook hands; there were no more armed guards to keep us apart. They came with gifts of food, clothing, soap, and other unheard-of luxuries. They came with accordions and harmonicas and brought song and laughter into our grim surroundings.

They brought us friendship and the gift of life. For it was Pierre and a group of his men who searched the barracks for explosives. And we watched, breathless and tense, as the wires and dynamite set up for our destruction came out bit by bit, stick after stick. We had refused to seek safety outside while these men endangered their lives for us. After what seemed an eternity their job was completed, and then *Voila! Vive la liberté!* we shouted together again and again. "Long live Freedom!" we shouted in a multitude of languages, and the barracks' walls resounded with the words they had never heard.

We sang together prayers of thanksgiving, hymns, anthems, and folk songs, while the music came louder and louder, livelier and livelier. Soon dancing began, and those of us too weak to join in watched in elation while eating like fiends; and everything had the sweetness of sugar, the sweetness that will stay in my mind forever as the taste of freedom. God, it was like a wonderful dream! It was unbelievable, and we wept and we laughed, eager to forget the agony of suffering.

But how can one forget?

I began to feel terribly alone in this happy crowd; the futility of it all seemed unbearable. The door to freedom was open at last. There were no fixed bayonets between me and the beautiful world outside, but I had no home to go back to and no future to look forward to. For almost six years I had struggled to survive, to see the enemy defeated; and now in the midst of the victory celebration, I suddenly realized that I had outlived my parents, my sisters, my brothers, and old friends. I was only twenty-three, but I felt old and filled with bitterness. Everything I loved was buried under a mountain of ashes in the crematory of Auschwitz. There was only hate left now and thoughts of revenge. Was there any other reason for living than to avenge the lost lives, the inhuman suffering—an eye for an eye? Oh God, how many eyes?

I looked at Mathilde, and I saw a quivering, contemptible creature before me. I looked hard. She was the embodiment of evil. How I hated her! I was drowning in hate. It dominated me as it dominated the crowd that had gone with Pierre in the morning and hunted her down in the cellar where she was hiding, as it dominated the crowd that gathered around them when they returned with her to the camp.

Pierre and a few elder women from the camp were conferring on the side, trying to decide what to do with Mathilde. Then they gave her a mop and a pail and told her to clean up the mess left after the celebration. She began to scrub. She went down on her knees and scrubbed, and the crowd followed her everywhere in the barracks, the kitchen, the latrines; and Andre with his accordion accompanied her, playing her beloved songs, *Deutschland über alles* and *Lili Marlene* over and over again. He played incessantly, and the crowd loved it. It was good to see the enemy humbled, the proud Mathilde on her knees. Hating was so easy, and hating with a crowd has a special appeal. I was fascinated as I looked at the spectacle. I was too fascinated to take an active part in it. I just watched at first, and the picture I saw has been haunting my nightmares ever since. The faces around me were like a blurred, moving mass; the voices floated in the vacuum of my brain. I was numb, devoid of all connection with feeling and thought. The only reality was hate—hate and Mathilde. She was on the floor sobbing as she scrubbed obediently, foot by foot, just as I did under her rule. But that wasn't all. That wasn't all, for suddenly someone produced a whip and began to beat her. I heard her scream, and it sounded just as we had screamed under her lashes.

It seemed all so easy—an eye for an eye, a scream for a scream. And then—and then I felt the whip pressed into my hand and heard a hoarse voice urging, "It's your turn now. Beat her!"

I felt cold sweat trickling down my back. My hand was limp; I couldn't move.

"Strike her! Strike her hard!" repeated the voice, and I heard the others snicker: "Do it! Are you a coward? Have you forgotten your parents? Have you forgotten how your people died?"

The fires of the Auschwitz smokestacks seemed to burn inside me. I was gasping for breath, and through the black smoke before my eyes I saw Mathilde. I raised my hand with the whip in it, the very same riding crop she had used on my back. I raised my hand, and with all the strength I had I brought it down on her.

"This is for my father!" My voice sounded thick.

A swish of the whip in the air, an ugly smacking sound, and there was Mathilde's flesh on the other end. "Revenge is sweet." Where had I heard that?

Again, deliberately and with great effort, I struck. "This is for my mother!" I heard myself say. My throat felt tight and hot, and a bitter taste was on my tongue.

"Go on!" urged the crowd, "Strike again for your brothers and sisters." Oh, yes, I had a long way to go. For my brothers, my sisters, the many friends and my own mixed-up life. All because of this louse and vermin like her.

The lust to hurt and destroy gave me strength. I could be just as hateful and brutal as they could. It only depended on which side of the whip one was. *Ach du Lieber Augustin* came gaily from Andre's accordion and excitement rose to a frenzy.

The crowd was waiting for the next blow, and down at my feet Mathilde was waiting, too. I met her eyes and for a sickening instant there was this silent understanding between us. We were on an equal level now. I felt bound to her! The thought made me hesitate.

"Come on," the spectators screamed. "This is what we've been waiting for."

"This?" The answer came from my very guts. I flung the whip into a corner. "No!" I tried to fight nausea and I welcomed the tears that suddenly streamed down my face; I needed that curtain between me and the crowd.

Finding my way out of the tight circle, I heard their contempt. "What's the matter with you, you weakling!"

I didn't stop to explain. It took me a long time to understand it myself.

Picture taken by Major Clarence L. Benjamin just as prisoners being transported by train saw Allied tanks and realized they had been liberated.

The Reunion

"THE WAR CAN'T LAST FOREVER," Father had said when the separations began, "and when it's over, we will meet at home."

Dora felt the gentle rocking of the train and her body vibrated with excitement. Home came nearer and nearer as the wheels swallowed the miles with rhythmic speed. She pressed her face to the window and the Polish countryside greeted her with the reassuring familiarity of an old friend.

"My God, nothing seems to have changed here," she thought. She had expected to find devastation, everything in ruins, but before her stretched gentle green pastures and pale gold wheat ripening in the sun under an almost iridescent sky. There was no rubble, but whitewashed farm buildings against the rich foliage of the orchards. Low roofs hung like eyebrows, and the windows under them twinkled in the bright sun.

"Soon," Dora mused, "the train will pass the big bend

in the road, and then I'll be home." For five years she had visualized her homecoming, never quite believing it would happen. She had dreamed it down to the smallest detail—the meeting with the family, the warm embraces, the exclamations. It seemed odd that now, at the end of her long journey, the picture eluded her so persistently. She could not recall any of the well-loved faces of the past, only the flames that had shot from the chimneys at Auschwitz and the veil of smoke that had hung over the camp.

Somehow, she had survived. Perhaps... Was it not possible that the others, too, were alive? "We'll meet again at home," Father's words echoed as if in answer. The war in Europe had been over and she had been liberated from the camp for some time, but the Red Cross doctor had refused to let Dora travel until the cast that encased her leg was removed. It was difficult to wait and Dora had wanted to start for home weeks ago, but she was grateful now for the delay. She would not want any of the family to see her limp. Besides, by being late she had probably given all the others the chance to reach home before her.

"Castle Street, Castle Street Depot!" bellowed the train conductor amid the clanging of the bell. Startled out of her daydreams, Dora jumped to her feet, adjusted the straps of her knapsack, and ran toward the entranceway. She realized that the passengers were looking at her curiously and wondered why they turned away when she met their gaze. "Why do they avoid looking into my face?" she asked herself. "They seem so embarrassed. Surely they must have seen others returning from concentration camps." And then Dora suddenly became conscious of her appearance—the too-large men's shoes which were all that could be found for her, the faded, dusty purple of the once-blue dress hanging loosely on her skinny body, the babushka on her scarecrow head, and the knapsack with her few belongings. She must look odd, indeed.

The fiery July sun almost blinded Dora as she stepped from the train. Pausing for a moment, she squinted down the lovely street that lay before her. The memory of the sparkling winter day when she had left Castle Street returned to her sharply. The street had been called Schloss Strasse then, and flags emblazoned with bold swastikas had hung from its buildings. The boulevard had swarmed with German soldiers. Victorious and boisterous, some loitered in groups, snapped pictures, while others marched, grinding the fresh snow into a squeaky carpet under their heavy boots.

She remembered how conspicuous and humiliated she had felt wearing the yellow Star of David sewn to her clothes and how Father had repeated over and over again, "The shame is on those who make us wear them." The seventeen year-old girl she was then had found it hard either to understand or to accept.

Now, quiet and almost deserted in the midday heat, Castle Street looked comfortingly serene again. The swastikas were gone, and the neon Eagle of Poland was back on the castle wall, spreading his wings as proudly as ever.

Letting her childhood memories guide her, Dora began the walk down the broad boulevard toward home. The church steeple didn't seem as tall as she remembered it; the stream under the little bridge looked narrower; the ancient castle was less awesome, and the large park beyond it that had always seemed so mysterious beckoned temptingly green and cool as ever.

The shops in the street looked as if the displays in their windows had not been changed in the five years of her absence; only the signs above the doors bore unfamiliar names. In Mr. Markus' apothecary shop, the tall jars of green and yellow liquid still guarded the white porcelain mortar and pestle between them, but the shingle now read: "Morawski." "Cohen's Grocery" had been changed to "Stanislaw Kowalczy." In place of "Bakery—G. Salz," a big new sign read "Fresh Breads—Slovik."

She was glad there were so few people along the way, for those she passed bore that same look of embarrassment that had puzzled her on the train. Mr. Slovik stood in front of his bakery but turned his flour-dusted face away as he saw Dora approaching.

Presently she passed the bank and thought of its cool,

polished interior and of Mr. Yablonski, the bank president. She recalled that he had told Father, shaking his hand: "We need more men like you on the City Council, Mr. Bornstein." There was a time, Dora remembered, smiling inwardly, when she considered Mr. Yablonski the handsomest man in the world, next to Father, of course.

A little farther down, on the corner of Pulaski Street, Dora looked into the tiny newsstand, hoping to see old Mr. Kubiak, who had owned it for as long as she could remember. But instead she saw a stranger, an old man dozing while the thick, black headlines around him screamed of fighting somewhere in the Pacific islands.

Dora crossed the street and stopped for a moment at the spot where, coming home from school with her friend, Ida, they would engage in the daily ritual of parting. The voices seemed to linger there still. "Will you come to my house today?" Ida would ask. And Dora would always reply: "I might have to come. My mother might be having another baby today!" Their large family was a familiar and appreciated joke, and the Bornsteins laughed along with everybody else. Father, too, used to have fun with the subject. He would point at one of the children from his seat at the head of the table, his eyes laughing behind his glasses, and say, "You, down there"; and, as they nodded in turn, "No, not you—I mean the one with the braids; what was your name again?"

With a flash of bitter recollection, Dora remembered

her long, thick braids. A shudder ran through her as her thoughts took her back to the barracks in Auschwitz, and she again felt the cold touch of the clippers against her scalp. She pulled the babushka down over her forehead until it covered her new, inch-long crop of hair and quickened her step.

She started down Pulaski Street, and there it was—Number 12, the house where she had been born and raised, stood unchanged. Dora saw the balcony facing the street and recalled Father leaning over the railing, shouting to the jubilant crowd below the big news he had heard on the radio: "France and England are fighting on our side! The war will be over in no time now." That happened a few days after the invasion had begun. Was it only six years ago?

The street was empty now but for two girls playing hopscotch. They stopped only long enough to look at Dora with their mouths open. She could hear them laughing behind her as she passed them.

A woman called the little girls from a window above, and they ran into their house still giggling. It was time for the midday meal, and the clatter of dishes and the murmur of contented voices wafted through the open windows.

Dora was uncomfortably aware of curious eyes peering at her from behind the curtains, but no one called out to her as she passed. As she ran up the stairs two at a time, her legs skipping certain steps, just as she had always done, she could almost see Mother smiling at the door, softly admonishing: "Won't you ever learn to walk up these stairs like a lady? When are you going to grow up?"

The ring of the bell sounded loudly in the cool darkness of the hall, and Dora's tongue felt dry and thick as she tried to moisten her parched lips. The wild thumping of her heart filled her chest.

After an eternity, the door opened and a woman's voice called: "What do you want?" Then, as Dora stood speechless, it demanded: "Who are you?" A head of tightly curled ringlets appeared in the doorway, framing a middle-aged face. Gray eyes regarded Dora curiously while the woman's hands, caked with dough, adjusted an enormous apron.

"I used to live here," the girl found words, "before the war. I've come back now, and I hoped perhaps the others, too..."

The woman shook her head slowly and moved to close the door when Dora asked, "May I come in, please, just for a little while?" The flicker of sympathy in the gray eyes gave way to growing suspicion, but the woman stepped aside reluctantly. "All right, come in—but if you want anything, you'll have to talk to my husband."

"She's probably afraid that I've come to claim my possessions," Dora thought as she entered the apartment.

She was painfully conscious of the stillness of the rooms as she looked into them. The roses on the wallpaper looked somewhat faded, but some of the furniture was still there, shining and polished as she remembered it. And the lace curtains hung softly, with the shadow of the pear tree in the yard superimposed on their design. Coming closer to the window, Dora saw the old bench beneath the fruit-laden tree and tried to recall the last book she had read sitting there.

In the dining room, Father's leather-bound volumes had been replaced by a collection of animal figurines staring at her from behind the glass doors of the bookcase. The eight matching chairs stood in perfect symmetry around the long oaken table, and Dora thought of the everyday scramble when four chairs from the kitchen had had to be brought in to seat the family at mealtime.

With the woman following her closely, Dora touched the shining surface of the table, lingering where each member of her family had sat for so many years.

There was Father with his gentle humor, ready to share his learning and his smile, saying, as she had heard so often: "Goodness is the strongest force in the world, and God loves goodness more than piety." ... And Mother, the beautiful queen of Dora's childhood, the perfect lady, whose energy was matched only by her unbounded optimism and faith in people. ... Then Grandmother Pearl, little old granny with the big heart.

Weekly, she would order the baker to make huge loaves of bread and dispatch Dora and her sisters on errands of mercy to the poor. ... Celina, the eldest sister, readying her trousseau, her fingers nimbly embroidering the pillowcases with tiny, loving stitches. ... Sara, the poetess with green, dreamy eyes, who penned romantic odes and humorous verse. ... Aram, the big brother, poring over his stamp collection. ... And Luba, the delightful clown of the family, who could make them laugh any time without half trying. ...

Dora stood wordlessly. Her breath was coming fast, and her lips were slightly parted, as if inhaling the memories that became so clear at last. She heard water dripping from a faucet and the ever-present staccato of the big clock on the wall, mingled with laughter, talk, and songs of the past.

There was Zalman practicing his violin lessons, playing over and over his favorite *Träumerei* until it came out their ears. ... Next to him, Bronia, who had spent months in a dark room recovering from an eye infection. Everyone had taken turns playing with her until she could emerge into the light, her blue eyes more beautiful than ever. ... Teen-age Guta, primping before the mirror for endless hours and claiming that no one understood her, was always late to the dinner table. ... Little Esther, the baby of the family, pampered and spoiled by them all, always had to be hauled away from her post, gazing at the birds' nest on the balcony.

"The swallows!" Suddenly remembering the nest under the eaves, Dora turned to the woman and asked, "Would you mind if I went out onto the balcony?" Nodding in agreement, the woman followed her as she passed through the big bedroom where the family often gathered after curfew that first winter of war. This room was the easiest to keep warm, and together they had sat around the huge, white-tiled fireplace, listening to Zalman read aloud from the many books on the shelves.

The floor of the balcony used to be covered with paper to catch the bird droppings; the concrete was hot and white now under Dora's feet. There, under the eaves, a patch of poorly matched paint marked where the nest had been. "What happened to the birds?" the girl asked. "They used to come back every spring."

"I don't know," the housewife replied. "They weren't here when I moved in and I don't know anything about them. Maybe my husband could tell you." She edged Dora toward the door. "Come back when he is home if you want something."

"Thank you for letting me in," Dora said softly. "I won't bother you any more. I had to come back to find them, to know…" Tears rose in her throat. "I hoped, you see…" Her voice broke, and she turned hurriedly from the woman. Without looking back, she murmured again a blurred "Thank you" and left the apartment. She heard the door click gently behind her as, step by painful step, she began to walk down the stairs.

The tree-lined street lay still and drowsy in the midday heat. The knapsack felt heavy on her shoulders, and she was suddenly very thirsty. On her way back to the depot, Dora stepped carefully over the chalk marks of the children's game on the sidewalk.

Editor's Note:

When I read "The Reunion" to school groups, I often ask, "Do you think my mother actually went back to her childhood home? If so, why does she tell the story from the perspective of someone named Dora?" I wish I knew the answers.

I do know that my mother uses the actual names of her family members throughout the story. Dora's father is Mr. Bornstein, as was my mother's father. As Dora recalls her brothers and sisters, she reminisces about them one at a time, and their names are those of my mother's siblings. I suspect that the character traits and hobbies she mentions truly described them.

Dora's destination is 12 Pulaski Street, and I know that this was my mother's childhood address in Pabianice, Poland. Recall that Dora disembarks from the train at the Castle Street station. To this day, there is a train station called "Zamkowa-Zamek" ("zamek" being the Polish word for "castle"), an eight-minute walk from what had been the Bornstein's home on Pulaski Street.

It is possible that my mother made the trip back home but found it too painful to tell the story in the first person. It is also possible she never returned home and that the story describes what she imagined might have occurred if she had.

The World Holocaust Remembrance Center, Yad Vashem, refers to survivors journeying home as Dora did, noting that "returning Polish Jews encountered an antisemitism that was terrible in its fury and brutality." The most shocking such episode was the Kielce pogrom of July 4, 1946, in which 42 returning survivors were murdered by their former neighbors. According to Yad Vashem, this "sounded an internal alarm: during the months that followed it, survivors fled from Eastern Europe any way they could." The Kielce massacre was one of many documented incidences of postwar anti-Semitic violence, and it seems safe to say that many who survived the Holocaust resisted the urge to return home and instead sought homes in safer environs.

Whether or not my mother traveled back to Pabianice, it is my hope that each of the Bornsteins will (as in "The Reunion") be remembered as individuals, each with his or her own dreams, pastimes, and personalities.

∾

Wedding photo of Felicia and Abram Lubliner, 1946

Afterword

Don't ask. Don't tell.

These words seem applicable to a set of unspoken rules that existed in my household as I was growing up. Wanting me to have a normal life, to think of myself as someone with unlimited potential and not a victim, and to enjoy the freedom gained by emigrating to the United States, my parents focused on the "here and now," not delving into their pasts when speaking to me. This meant not talking about the family members they had lost, which included my grandparents, uncles, and aunts. The names of these people were not spoken in our household, and, as a result, I know almost nothing about them.

I wish I could help you, the reader, get to know my mother, but I feel as if I hardly know her myself. She passed away 45 years ago, and my memories have faded with time. She tried so hard to give me a normal upbringing, to shelter me from anything that would resemble her own shattered childhood. I think she was waiting until

I was older, more mature, and curious to learn about her younger years, my deceased relatives, and what she endured in the camps. Had she lived longer, I'd have eventually reached that point, but this was not to be.

When my mother died, there were so many questions left unanswered. I wonder why I never asked them. Is it because I, a rebellious teenager, was trying to keep my distance from her? Is it because I was too self-absorbed to ask my mother to tell me about her Holocaust experiences? Is it because I knew, on some deep level, that getting her to talk about those ordeals would dredge up horrific memories and trigger pain? Looking back, I think that all those things played a part in my not speaking up, asking the many questions I would ask if she were alive today.

Do ask. Do tell.

If there are older members of your family still alive, ask them to share their stories with you. There will come a time when it is too late. To ask about their younger days is to honor their experience and to say to them, "I really want to know you. I want the deeper connection with you that will come from knowing about your life experiences and our shared ancestry. By better understanding you and those who came before you, I will better understand myself."

If there are younger members of your family—your children, grandchildren, nieces or nephews—seek what educators call the "teachable moments," the situations in which young ones are really listening and receptive to learning. The stories about your own childhood, about relatives that are no longer alive or live far away, and about the world you knew growing up, will enrich the lives of the next generation, helping them to understand where they came from and who they really are.

A few weeks before she died, my mother recorded some of her innermost thoughts on a cassette tape, most of which were about her fears of death. I recently played that recording and heard her say to me:

> "I'm afraid of nothingness. I'm afraid of not being. Not being! What am I going to leave behind? ... How long will I be remembered? How long? For as long as one is remembered, one is not dead. I believe that. You can live in people's minds, memories, and hearts. I believe that."

As I heard those words, I was reminded of a letter that I received from a high school student with whom I had shared my mother's writing. This student wrote:

> "Keep doing what you're doing. When you share her stories, you will not only be honoring your mother, but you will change so many different lives."

By guiding her writing into your hands, I have faith that my mother will live on in your mind, your memory, and your heart, as she does in mine. May this book serve as a fitting tribute to her indomitable spirit and resilience. That is my only hope.

I miss you, Mom.

Appendices

Felicia Lubliner in the early 1970s

Presentation at San Francisco State University, 1967

FELICIA LUBLINER: Many books have been written on the subject of Holocaust, and undoubtedly you have read most of them by now.

There were, 20 years ago, millions of dead in Europe. Six million of them were Jews. Did you ever find a trace of identification with a person among those six million? How many Anne Franks have longed, have suffered, and died in this multitude?

The six million have been collectively explained, condemned, extolled as martyrs. They have been analyzed, but collectively.

Auschwitz was a strange place. Sorry. *[weeps]* No one that has not been in Auschwitz—I don't think anybody can really understand what it was like. I would like you then to go back with me into a past, and try, if you will, to picture yourself in my shoes, so to speak, if I had any.

Try, in fact, to think, if you can, if you will, that it was you. Just you. How would you feel? How would you behave? Would you have attacked an SS guard with your bare hands, as it was suggested in certain books that the prisoners should have done?

Would you have committed suicide rather than prolong the agony, the misery, and humiliation? What would you have done?

It's 1939, vacation is over, and you had plans to go back to school. You thought you will become a teacher someday, perhaps. Then the bombs fly over your head. It doesn't take long. The victorious German army marches into your town. And a little short while after that, you're forced to move out from the home where you were born, and raised, and been happy, and dreamed—to a ghetto. Cramped quarters, but you're with your family, and you learn.

In three years, sometimes two, sometimes four, as the case was, there was a process of learning, despite the fact that your formal education was interrupted. You learn many things in a ghetto.

You learn to value your privacy. You learn to value food. You learn that hunger is not in your belly; it's a burning hole in your brain. *[lights a cigarette]*

You learn to step over dead bodies in the streets. You learn to wash potato peelings, when you get them, in the ice, the icy water, till your hands get dry and raw. You learn not to move a muscle when bayonets go through a bed where your mother is hidden. You learn to steal, to grab, to grab a potato under a barrage of bullets. You learn many things in a ghetto.

And then, someday you also learn to part with your friends, with members of the family. Gradually, one by one, the family gets smaller, and you think they are probably in another ghetto. They work. You learn to work very hard. You learn to count every bite that you eat.

But you hope. There are rumors in the ghetto. There are people running around with news—the German army's been conquered; they're taken a beating at every front; the war cannot last much longer. So you hope. Someday it will all end, that you'll go back to normal life; you'll just pick up where you left.

Then one day, an announcement: "The ghetto has to be evacuated because we need you to work, but in a different place, to support our war effort, and it will do us good, and that's where you will remain alive, and we will win the war." You don't want the Germans to win the war, but you do want to stay alive.

And besides, what have you got to lose here? It's getting worse to worse. Your feet are swelling; you touch them—they throb from hunger. Your body begins to swell. What have you got to lose? What could be worse, really?

So when the orders come, and, of course, everything has to be very orderly—we don't want any disturbances on the part of the Jewish population; take your belongings;

Deportation

volunteer. And do you know, you think, perhaps I *should* volunteer. After all, we're going to be resettled. And we're going to be given conditions—they would not *dream* of doing anything worse. What *could* be worse? But no, you've learned to mistrust the rumors, good and bad. You don't volunteer. If they want you, they have to come and take you.

And there is a knock at the door—when you think you are bolted in from the outside by your neighbors safely—there is a knock at the door, and they are here to get you. And speechlessly, quietly, facing the barrel of the gun, you pick up your bundle, your suitcase, and you go.

You come to a train station; you're being told to get on it. You don't know where, probably to another ghetto. You're given a loaf of bread, and you're told it's going to be alright. You board the train, a cattle train. You hear the seals locking from the outside and begin to move.

The train is packed; there are bodies around you. You fight for breath. You try to push away, make a little room around you. It's impossible. What do you think in a cattle train, going to a destination unknown? Well, you think about the potato you left at home you could have taken along. You think of—you don't think what you're facing, you don't think about it at all. But there's speculations. There are perennial pessimists that will tell you, "Oh, they're going to kill us all."

On the other hand, there is a very rational explanation. Now, why really, would anybody want to kill us? We're useful. We can work; they need us. You see, in spite of everything you've learned in the ghetto, you had not learned about the "Final Solution" of the Jews. You don't know what's going on because you didn't have a paper; you didn't have a radio. You were shut off; you had no contact with the world. You did not know.

And the train moves on, and it's getting hot. You try to fight your way towards the bucket of water. And you're denied every swallow of it because there's so many that want that water. There are children urinating and

Cattle car used to transport prisoners to Auschwitz

defecating all around you. A makeshift curtain is erected. How do you feel when you have to perform your call of nature in front of strangers for the first time?

But the train moves on endlessly. You're jostled against the bodies. You're beginning—after a while, you get numb. You don't function. Then the train stops.

Strange place. It's a strange place you see when the door finally opens. There is a gate over which there is the legend *Arbeit macht frei*; that is "Work sets you free." Only later, you realize that the gate should have said, "Abandon all hope, ye who enter here."

And you enter, and there is a reception committee for you, complete with guns, bayonets, dogs. A band is blaring in the distance, and a voice from a loudspeaker, very comfortably, very reassuringly telling you, "Leave your belongings in the car. Get out. Haste, *schnell*, hurry."

The older people and the children who cannot work

will have to go to the left, to another camp. The younger people will go to the right. And so you separate. And you have no time to think because all this is done in such a hurry, everything, *schnell*! And you don't think. You're just a bundle of reflexes, so you separate from your mother. You have no time to wonder where she's gone.

And then you are put in rows of five, and you march down the street. You still clutch the little piece of bread that's left, what they gave you when you boarded the train, and you enter a new world.

You see rows, of rows, of rows, of rows of wires crisscrossing the site in every direction. You march along a walk between barracks, and in front of these barracks there are people standing, strange-looking people, with uniforms like pajamas, striped. Shaven, mostly men, grinning at you saying, "You're new here, but you'll get adjusted. It's not going to be too bad; you'll get used to it." You don't think. You think of your mother, you think of her eyes, and you wonder: What did she try to tell you when you left her on the left side? But you don't know what happened to her.

And you walk down the street, and through the wires you see creatures out of a different—oh, you think this is an insane asylum; these people must be insane, and that's why they're kept behind wires. They're creatures like scarecrows, running around in rags, barefoot, shaven. But with a close look, you see they're women. And they run around; they come as close to the wire as they can, and shout at you.

And at first you don't understand, and you strain, and you try to understand what they're telling you. And they shout, "Throw your bread. They'll take it away!" And you don't believe them; you think they're insane. So you clutch the piece of bread and you walk down.

You're taken to a barracks, ordinary-looking barracks, nothing. You're told to strip, to put all your—and you still carry your pictures, your papers, with you. Put everything aside and strip completely. You're going to obey. You don't think much; you follow. You strip. You stand naked in front of men. Women stand naked in front of men, and men stand naked in front of women. And somehow you don't feel shame for yourself, even though it's a terrible thing, especially if you're young, because you don't consider these people really men, these people that are around you, the guards. You don't consider them men after a while, or women. They are just SS; they don't count, really. But it hurts, just the same.

You walk down the line. There's a barber, removing all the hair from your body. You emerge on the other side, driven into a cold, ice-cold shower. You come out; they don't give you anything to dry yourself with, of course. And you stand there and you look at the people around you, the people that you've known all your lives. And you begin to laugh hysterically because they look so very funny, all these girls without hair, naked, shivering. It's hysterical, really! So you laugh, you laugh yourself till you cry.

And then you're driven outside, and you're thrown a rag which doesn't fit you, perhaps a blouse that's too short, a skirt that's too long, and that's all. No underwear. You grab it, you put it on, and you're told to stand; you're going to be counted.

You stand for hours. You think you're going to die every minute you stand there, but you don't die. You stand, and you're counted. And you are being brought to barracks, another long structure with stalls on each side and a little brick chimney right through the center, about three feet high. And you're told to sit in rows of five, straddling the next person in front of you, and so on, in rows of five.

And this is how you are going to sit for the next month. This is how you're going to sleep. If one of these five have to turn, the rest of them will turn with you. You have no privacy; you have nothing left. There's one blanket, if you're lucky, for five. There is one pot of watery soup handed out to you once a day, for five. And when you take a sip of this pot of soup, there are four hungry eyes following you, and every swallow that you take is counted.

You try to sleep later. The door bursts open, and a strange creature comes in, runs up and back and front on the fireplace that runs across and says, "You are here to obey orders. By time I get through with you, you will know what I mean" and things of that nature. You don't care at this point. You just wanted to be left alone. But in Auschwitz you're not alone, ever. There are crowds around you, shuffling feet, bodies. You are driven to the latrine in a group. If you want to wash on your own, you have to risk your life at night, and run. If you're caught, you die clean. But there is no—you have only one thing left. That's your life, your *bare* life. And your spirit. And this is what you try to keep, your life and your spirit.

To remain human in Auschwitz was probably the greatest effort that you've ever faced in your life. *[lights a cigarette]* To remain a human in spite of the dehumanization that was going on, that you watched every day, took all the strength you had left. This, and to remain alive, and there was a struggle. Every hour spent in Auschwitz alive was a victory.

You had two choices. People have been—certain authors have suggested and asked the question, "Why haven't the prisoners staged a revolt? Why haven't they attacked the SS? Even bare-handed, it would have been better than dying in a chamber."

Well, it probably sounds very good. If you had by now felt a little bit of it, and if you know what it is to look—when you are barefoot, to look at the person who has shoes on, just try that once. The Nazis had a system when they took fresh prisoners, they took their shoes away, make them walk barefoot. It's humiliation in that.

You look into this barrel of a gun and you think, "I'm going to attack it," and they ask the question, what would happen? Well, it's a foolish way of committing suicide because it would have been murder, as well. You would jeopardize the lives of the others around you, the lives that they're so desperately trying to save. The lives that were left to us as a legacy by those that were hanged. Their last words were, "Keep on living. Hang on. Carry on." No, attacking the guards was not an answer.

On the contrary, you did not move away from the crowd; you did not try to single yourself out because there was danger in being alone. You had safety, after a while, in a crowd.

You could also try another method. You could commit suicide; you could take your own life. You could have spared the SS the effort. Death was cheap at Auschwitz. It looked at you. It stank its way into your very brain. It looked at you from the eyes of the condemned, from the eyes of the examining doctor who made the selections. It sang its weird song on the wires at night. That was really a temptation. You felt as if you wanted to touch the wires, and in one second you'd be out of all this.

No, no, you would choose to live, and wait, and hope. And you'd go back to the barracks and face it, for another day, for another hour. It cannot last forever. And if you had lost in the end, you'd march to your death with the others. In silence in which, contrary to all you might have heard, was dignity. A silence which shouted, shrieked a mute protest into the heavens, unheeding heavens, and into a mute world, deaf world. So we chose to live. These are the only two choices you had.

Who are some of the people that you met in Auschwitz? There is a girl next to you. She was an artist before the war, sculpture. Sculpture was her life. It still was her life in Auschwitz. With her shaven head, shaven naked skull, and white skin, and skinny legs, and with her incongruous rag that she was given, which was in wild colors, she looked like a butterfly, and she was called "Butterfly."

This girl managed to save a little piece of bread every day from her ration, which was small enough. She saved the bread, and she kneaded it into a little ball and made figurines out of it, the most exquisite pieces of art you would wish to find. She took grains of sand and took great, great pains to find the right color to make eyes for these figurines. She died; she was taken away clutching one of those figurines in her hand. They didn't kill her, really. They killed her body. But they couldn't kill her spirit.

So you live on day after day, and you hope. There is always hope. You learn that people are capable of inflicting pain that seems unbearable. And on the other side of the spectrum, people are capable of receiving and bearing pain which seems unbearable. You learn that to be a hero, one does not have to wear the shining armor. And one can be a coward, armed to the teeth. [Sound on recording breaks up, indicated from now on with ...].

You learn many things. You learn to be proud. You learn to look into the eyes of the SS when they beat you, when they hit you. You look them straight in the eyes and think to yourself, "I am better. I am better than you." This is a hard lesson, but you learn it because you feel it, you know it. This helps you, in a way, as you sit and wait, and wait, for the tomorrow that might never come.

And then there are those chimneys, which at first look so reassuringly like a factory. And all the while, you wonder. You see the smoke. You see the fire pouring out. You feel the stench. At first you ask questions: What is being burned there? What is being manufactured there? The first answers you hear: it's a factory; they work. Next, when this you feel this is not sufficient, you begin to ask more questions. You find out or you get answers: "Our clothes are being burned there. Our papers are being burned there. Our hair is being burned there." *Everything* is being burned there, but not your mother, because you can't believe it. It's too monstrous. So you try not to believe it. You have no way of really knowing until you go there, and when you go there and find out, now it's too late.

And you think, and at night you meet a woman. She was a dentist before the war, but she studied in Kiev, so she had a group of people around her; she taught them Russian at Auschwitz.

There was another one. She was an opera singer before the war. She sang. Books that you have read before, poems that you knew before, ideas that you had before were discussed and shared with others. You talked a lot about your past. You hung on to it. Because that was the real, concrete thing you could hang on to. Because there was no future. And today, now, was too unbelievable to be true.

How would you feel in this unreal world, could you imagine? It is not really real, it doesn't happen, it couldn't be happening. You sometimes think it's a different planet. That it isn't really you that's there.

And then there is a final selection. You never know which way to run, because one selection will take away the young people, and one selection will take away the middle-aged people. The one will take away the ones that look—still have a little flesh on your bones; the other selection will come and take the real skeleton-like people. So you don't know who they are going to pick and in which group to find shelter. So you rub a little brick into your cheeks to look healthier; perhaps you'll pass. There will be another day. And by tomorrow, the war might be over.

You march in front of the doctor. The band is playing. He is whistling a tune. You pass in front of him. He looks at you. You're naked, of course. With a wave of his hand, he decides your fate. *Rechts, links. Rechts, links.* Not until the vans come and take away a group do you really know which group is going where, and where you're going to go.

Then we watch the vans going away, packed with bodies, and you see eyes, hundreds of eyes, looking at you silently, moving away. What is the message? You see people from the vans taking off their shoes—that's if they manage to have any—to throw them back to the ones that were left. They won't be needing them anymore. And then you fight for those shoes to get them, if you're left.

So it's a struggle. But if you had preserved one spark of your identity, of what you were, or wanted to be, you have won. Dead or alive, you have won.

And then, if you're lucky—although at that time you don't think you're lucky; you don't know it—you survive the war. You find yourself alone, friendless, with no home. Nothing to go back to. And again, you dare not yet think of future, so you think of the past.

Now, you think of the immediate past and you're filled with bitterness. You're filled with hate, for everything, to the world that allowed this to happen. You hate yourself for having stayed alive while the others are dead. You think of the things you *might* have done, perhaps.

Could you have put a little more of the brick dust on your little sister? Perhaps it would help her. Perhaps she, too, would pass the selection. You think of these things.

You think of revenge. You think a lot of revenge. And you also think of filling your belly, of having enough to eat, of having clothes, and a toothbrush. And you have to make choices again. Are you going to go through your life without having learned anything? Are you going to turn out to be a bitter, hateful person? Or are you going to turn your mind and try to see the world, and yourself, objectively, and try to act and build a life that you think might be of some credit to you? You also think it might be of some credit to those that were not here to watch it. You learn, most of all, that human spirit is unconquerable. And if you had learned that and somehow feel, then perhaps your staying alive was worth it, all this.

Thank you.

PROFESSOR HALPERIN: Do you have some questions?

AUDIENCE MEMBER: How old were you at the time you moved?

FELICIA LUBLINER: How old? I was 17 when the war came, when the war started. I will be very glad to answer any of your questions, if you have any. Yes?

AUDIENCE MEMBER: A good number of the people who were responsible for what happened to you are now in power in Germany today. How do you feel about Germany?

FELICIA LUBLINER: Very uneasy. I feel that Germany today—let me phrase it the way I—I feel that the German people—now again, I speak of people collectively, which is possibly a mistake—they don't feel guilty, really. They don't identify the crimes against humanity or against Jews; they don't think of it as a crime.

I feel—and I felt that when I went back to Germany, after liberation when I had to live there for a while. There's people who professed they never knew anything about the killings and extermination who were wondering, "There's only few of you that came back." And I don't think that they ever got the full impact of it; they do not want to know. The people that lived through it want to forget […] I met some young people when I was in Paris years ago, I met a young German girl […], she ran away from home because she felt her parents were guilty, but they never wanted to discuss anything with her.

And I think that the German people—now I might say something that they would do should the chance come; they probably more or less would feel the same. I might be very prejudiced on such a thing.

Yes?

AUDIENCE MEMBER: Do you find that other people you know that are Jewish and have similar, or maybe escaped [...], do you find that they are active now in movements to remove social evil, like the civil rights struggle or the peace movement?

FELICIA LUBLINER: Yes, I feel more or less—I would say yes. You have to understand that the people that survived are a little bit, are the generation that they're parents now, they raise a family. They try to lead a normal life, and they try their [...]. However, I don't think that any person that has gone through this and has seen how hate can destroy the victims and the—what's the opposite of the victim?—the tormentor, alike. People like this cannot remain neutral.

I don't know just how many take an active part in the struggle for truth and freedom, but I know they identify themselves very strongly with these ideas. Does that answer your question?

AUDIENCE MEMBER: Yes.

PROFESSOR: You talked about revenge before. At an earlier point, we did discuss your experience with that. Would you mind talking about that experience?

FELICIA LUBLINER: Alright. Shall I just describe as it happened? The whole thing?

PROFESSOR: Yeah.

FELICIA LUBLINER: Well, the war was over. Let me first describe how it started, how it came about, at least to me. On May 8th of 1945, towards the evening, when we were usually counted, there was the commandant of the camp, or of the whole group of camps—now I would like to point out this was in a labor camp after Auschwitz. I was taken to work after all, not to the gas chambers, obviously—he came that May 8th, unforgettable evening, had us all lined up and said, "The war is ending. You are going to be free." And then he said, "Haven't I always been good to you?" And a chorus of voices because we quite—we thought it was a trick. We answered, "Yes, sir!" Of course, you never believe a German after a while. You learn not to believe him, a Nazi at least.

But it was true. They all disappeared, all the guards, overnight, disappeared, and so 600 women were left in this building alone, unprotected, in a strange world, in a strange town.

A little later at night, the door burst open, and a group of French people from a nearby French camp, who were known—we had known them because we worked side by side in the factory, but we were not supposed to talk to each other during the Nazi reign. But that night they came with the strangest thing. One of them brought a sack of sugar on his shoulders, a very heavy sack, and he put it down in the middle of the room. *Voila!* And we dipped our hands into the sugar, and we ate it, and we ate it, and we ate it, and we couldn't get enough of it! And there were shouts in French, and pretty soon the Italians came. And *Viva la liberté!* "Long live freedom!" And shouts and shaking hands. And I think that I like sugar ever since; it tastes like freedom.

And then they started—they had heard, or discovered, that before they escaped, the Nazis had laid out wires and dynamite to blow us up, a final gesture to their gods. Well, these wonderful French boys had dismantled the—whatever—they took out sticks of dynamite bit by bit. And after this, a celebration began, and accordions, and music, and shouting, and laughter, and crying, and embracing. It was a wild, wild night.

And we went into the SS quarters and got the portraits of Hitler and Himmler, and it was a great pleasure to step on them, and poke holes in them. And this went on, and on, and on. We didn't really reflect what it meant at this moment, freedom; it was just so sudden. And unbelievable, really, because it hit us. We wanted it, we waited for it, we hoped for it, and we struggled for it, but when it came, we were not prepared.

And then, a few days went by, and we had tried to adjust to it. There was no place we had to go yet, so we stayed within the confines and we burned every bit of the bunks to cook with it, to use for fuel and warmth. But it was, again, waiting. What to do next? What to do next?

Well, naturally, you wanted to go and find your

family. So these were the plans; you're waiting for the communication to be restored, for the trains to run. In the meantime, you went around to visit neighboring camps and hospitals. There were a lot of camps around the neighborhood, and people, men and women had worked there during the Nazi—

I happened to—I would like to tell you this—I went to see one of these hospitals in search of my family. And I found an old friend who studied—he came back from Paris where he studied during—but it was in the summer of '39, he had come back to Poland and then never managed to get back to Paris. I had known him as a vivacious, full-of-wit, sparkling person. And I'll never forget when I found him, he was a skeleton, a living skeleton, and the skin looked like parchment, stretched very tight on his bones. And he somehow recognized me. And I said, "Sigmund, can I get you something?" He said, "You know, my mother used to cook such good rhubarb. Could you get me some rhubarb?" Well, I went, searched, begged. I got the rhubarb. I cooked it for him. I brought it to him. He was dead. These are the things you encountered after the war. He made it to freedom, but only to the threshold.

And one day as I was standing in front of the barracks, I saw a group of people coming towards the camp, kind of a rugged, crazy, weird-looking group. Looking at them from the distance, they looked like insects swarming and swarming. Well, these were my inmates, my friends, from the camp, and they were marching towards me, and André was playing his accordion.

And there was somebody—they surrounded somebody, somebody in the circle. And I looked when they came close, and I recognized one of the guards, the camp leader, the SS. They tracked her down in a cellar, and they brought her. And she didn't look at all like the old Mathilde. Her pride was gone. They had shaven her hair, the French boys did, and she was caught wearing an old housedress and some slippers. To see Mathilde dressed like a woman, it was rather strange, because all I had known her was in a uniform with full regalia and insignia, with a whip, a riding crop in her hand, a revolver at her side, boots, long pageboy peroxide hair. That was Mathilde. She looked so different now. It was fascinating to see her. I couldn't get enough of it. I relished it, every minute, looking at Mathilde, down.

Well, she was brought to camp, and we didn't quite know what to do with her. So the French boys and a few of the older women decided at first, while they decide, they'll let her clean up the mess after the celebration. So, she was given a pail, a mop, and was driven to the latrine, and told to scrub. And scrub she did, just like we did before. It was really strange.

And the music, and André kept playing *Lili Marlene,"* and every song he could sing, and *Deutschland Über*

Alles to get Mathilde even—to get the contrast between those was just impossible, probably, to describe.

At any rate, somebody suddenly produced the whip, Mathilde's crop. And there was a circle around her as she scrubbed, and somebody began to beat her. And she screamed, and it was good to hear. And you felt, well, an eye for an eye, a scream for a scream. I was really fascinated with this at first. And I watched it without taking an active part in it till the whip was pressed into my hand, and a voice said, "It's your turn now. Beat her."

I was numb at first. And then the urging from the crowd, the mob, "Beat her! For your parents! For your sisters! Don't you remember your people? Don't you want to take revenge? Beat her!" I took the whip, and I lowered it. And there was Mathilde on the other side of it, and it felt good. And again, for my mother, for my father. And the crowd shouted, and André played. It was a frenzy; it was hysteria. I was part of it.

I enjoyed it at first. It was really good, till I looked at Mathilde down at my feet, and I caught her eye. And for a moment, for an instant, there was an understanding, as if an understanding between us. I was on her level. I could be just as brutal. I could be just as hateful. It only depended on which side of the whip I had happened to have been. Now the whip was in my hand. And the crowd urged, and André played *Ach du Leiber Augustin*, and they screamed, "Go on!"

I was ill. I was so revolted, I couldn't strike anymore. I flung the whip away, and I cried, and I walked away. And behind me, the crowd was saying, "What's the matter with her? What's the matter with you, you weakling?" I didn't stop to explain. It was a reflex; I didn't even realize it all myself at that time. But I think that this moment—at that moment, I had won the biggest struggle of my life. [lights cigarette]

Yes?

AUDIENCE MEMBER: You haven't said much about your religion, are you still an orthodox Jew?

FELICIA LUBLINER: I was raised in an orthodox family, and I grew away from it. For a while I was a complete atheist. I have a very different brand of religion, my own, which is very different from the religion that my father had.

My father had modern ideas, but, as far as religion was concerned, he was very orthodox, and we were raised that way. And I just can't accept religion as it was taught to me as a child after all this. So I don't consider myself—I am not an orthodox Jew. I don't know what kind of Jew I really am.

Yes?

PROFESSOR: With my own reaction to what you said, I think that there was some sort of a key regarding the spiritual strength, and the indomitable human strength, as it went through hell.

FELICIA LUBLINER: That's right.

PROFESSOR: And not having been there, outside of an event or in [...] of the religious framework, could you talk about the indomitable spirit, [...] where did it come from? I think that there is something about it that is lacking in this culture, in this society.

FELICIA LUBLINER: In our society here?

PROFESSOR: Yeah, and I don't know why, I think that [...] things might be a little better. I see signs of it at times, but other times I see its complete absence. But, out of your own experience from—where does the thing emerge?

FELICIA LUBLINER: Well, I can only tell you of my experience as a Jew, you see? That's the only experience I know. And, as a matter of fact, in very bitter times, the Jewish past, and the persecution, and the strength was mentioned, you know, the past, the Inquisition, and all the pogroms. And the strength was somehow derived from the fact that we were still a people, in spite of 2,000 years of exile, that we were still a people which could not be conquered by violence of any sort. I think that gave us a strength. The religious people, the ones that could remain religious in hell, drew their strength from that.

I remember Yom Kippur, you know, where the fast—the Jewish Day of Atonement and you're not supposed to eat anything—I think that this is probably the biggest thing I've ever seen in my life, a person in Auschwitz, where every bite of food or every swallow of the watery, sandy soup was your sustenance, and it could mean your life. People had to have a very strong faith, indeed, to not touch it on Yom Kippur, and give it away. There were people like that.

Now, it was a great help to rely on religion. There were people that went to—away with the *Shema Yisrael*, a cry which is "God is One." They never stopped believing. And that gave them strength.

And also what you were taught at home, you see. Well, I was taught, for instance—what helped me is my father's teachings of the basic goodness in mankind and man. Well, I'll give you an example. For instance, I will always remember—I don't know how much it will help you—but I remember when one of my youngest sisters was born, and my father and mother were almost out of names with so many of us, they were considering a name which implied "goodness."

> [Though the presentation continued, the recording ended at this point.]

Editor's Note:

I never met Doris Hobson or her family, but in 1992 she wrote a letter to the Holocaust Oral History Project to document conversations my parents had had with hers in Oakland, California. As my mother relates in her stories, Jewish prisoners were kept alive only as long as they could do work to assist the Nazi war effort. Until I received a copy of this letter from the Northern California Holocaust Center, I had no knowledge of the type of work that either of my parents did while in the concentration camps.

Though Doris Hobson passed away in 2003, this letter is reproduced here with the permission of her son, David Underwood of Citrus Heights, California. A more readable transcript of this letter appears on pages 111–113.

APRIL 12, 1992

Holocaust Oral History Project
639 14 Avenue
San Francisco, CA 94118

AVRAM AND FELICIA LUBLINER were in concentration camps, I do not know which ons and where they were liberated and the year.

My Mother, Deborah Hirshberg, was very active in Jewish affairs in Oakland. About 1950 the was an influx of Jews from concentration camps and my Mother assisted in finding homes for them. We became friendly with the Lubliners and now and then they would tell tales of there captivity. Two incidences I ramber very well.

Felicia was a taylor (she did beautiful work) and in the camp she was a seamstress. She was in line many times waiting her turn for the "ovens", but was always at the end of the line as she put it. Both hers and Avrams famxxsxxmxxx famalies were killed.
The captors began bringing to the seamstresses fur coats and heavy overcoats to be made into coats for the officers. At that time the women realized that Germany was going to invade Russia, so theysecretly made very fine razor blade cuts into the pelts before putting the lining on the inside of the coats. They reasoned if as they thought the Germans were going to invade in the winter and the snow was deep that the pelts would disintigrate when the soldiers walked in the deep snow.

She told when the camp was liverated by the Russians, the Russians turned the guards over to the prisoners, telling the prisoners they would be back in 3 or 5 days, do as they wished with their ex captors, but do not kill. The women guards were turned over to the women prisoners and they were lined up and whacked with boards or whatever they could find. Pushed them into the latrines and other punishments thry could think of. Felicia said she could not hit the women, but she did take their clothes and make them go naked.* She told me other stories, I did not ask, guess she just wanted to talk, but she usually shed tears as she told her stories. It embarrasessed me, and tho I did want to ask questions I did not ask, asshe would be upset, and we did not ever ask of her or Avram at any time, they would bring things up their selfs.

Avram was in the carpenter shops, and the men too realized or were told by the women that they thought the Germans were going in to Russia. They were given the task of building portable buildings which they realized would be barracks and other shelters for the troops. They secretly made doors and windows so they would not fit tightly when the buildings were assembled and other acts of sabotage as they were able to do. This so they would be harder to erect in the field, also that the cold air could seep thru the cracks. Avram's health was bad from his captivity, but he was able to always find work, his last job as an auto upholster, I do not know the company.

I was visiting in Oakland about 3 years ago and looked up Lubliner in the telephone book. XXxxMxxX They had one son born while I knew them and I have forgotten his first A woman answered the phone, did not have time to talk to me as she had an appointment, but she did tell me both of them had died. She was a relative, that is all I found out. I loved them both and so sorry I did not know of their death. I moved away to the foothills and lost touch, I do not remember which Jewish paper I read of your project, some time ago, hope this item is not too late for any research you are doing.

Sincerely,

Doris Hobson

Doris F. Hobson (Mrs R.P.)

* The women needed the clothes and had time to alter them for their return or release.

April 12, 1992

Holocaust Oral History Project
639 14 Avenue
San Francisco, CA 94118

AVRAM AND FELICIA LUBLINER were in concentration camps. I do not know which one and where they were liberated and the year.

My Mother, Deborah Hirshberg, was very active in Jewish affairs in Oakland. About 1950 the [sic] was an influx of Jews from concentration camps, and my Mother assisted in finding homes for them. We became friendly with the Lubliners, and now and then they would tell tales of there [sic] captivity. Two incidences [sic] I rember [sic] very well.

Felicia was a taylor [sic] (she did beautiful work), and in the camp she was a seamstress. She was in line many times waiting her turn for the "ovens," but she was always at the end of the line, as she put it. Both hers and Avram's families were killed.

The captors began bringing to the seamstresses fur coats and heavy overcoats to be made into coats for the officers. At that time, the women realized that Germany was going to invade Russia, so they secretly made very fine razor-blade cuts into the pelts before putting the lining on the inside of the coats. They reasoned if, as they thought, the Germans were going to invade in the winter and the snow was deep, that the pelts would disintegrate when the soldiers walked in the deep snow.

She told when the camp was liberated by the Russians, the Russians turned the guards over to the prisoners, telling the prisoners they would be back in 3 or 5 days, to do as they wished with their ex captors, but do not kill. The women guards were turned over to the women prisoners, and they were lined up and whacked with boards or whatever they could find. Pushed them into the latrines and other punishments they could think of. Felicia said she could not hit the women, but she did take their clothes and make them go naked.* She told me other stories. I did not ask; I guess she just wanted to talk, but she usually shed tears as she told her stories. It embarrasassed [sic] me, and tho [sic] I did want to ask questions, I did not ask, as she would be upset, and we did not ever ask of her or Avram at any time; they would bring things up their selfs [sic].

Avram was in the carpenter shops, and the men too realized or were told by the women that they thought the Germans were going in to Russia. They were given the task of building portable buildings which they realized would be barracks and other shelters for the troops. They secretly made doors and windows so they would not fit tightly when the buildings were assembled and other acts of sabotage as they were able to do, this so

---

* The women needed the clothes and had time to alter them for their return or release.

they would be harder to erect in the field, and also that the cold air could seep thru the cracks. Avram's health was bad from his captivity, but he was able to always find work, his last job as an auto upholster [sic]; I do not know the company.

I was visiting in Oakland about 3 years ago and looked up Lubliner in the telephone book. They had one son born while I knew them, and I have forgotten his first name. A woman answered the phone, did not have time to talk to me as she had an appointment, but she did tell me both of them had died. She was a relative; that is all I found out. I loved them both and so sorry I did not know of their death. I moved away to the foothills and lost touch. I do not remember which Jewish paper I read of your project, some time ago; hope this item is not too late for any research you are doing.

                Sincerely,
                Doris F. Hobson (Mrs. R.P.)

GLOSSARY

Atlas – In Greek mythology, Atlas and his brother Menoetius fought alongside the Titans in a war against the Olympians. When the Titans were defeated, Zeus condemned Atlas to the western edge of Gaia (the Earth), to hold up the heavens for eternity. In "The Reunion," Pierre appears carrying a large sack of sugar, and this was reminiscent of Atlas bearing the weight of the celestial spheres.

crematoria – Crematoria are buildings in which dead people's bodies are burned to ash (cremated). The singular form of the word is "crematorium." The Nazis disposed of bodies in many ways, cremation being one of them.

ersatz – This word refers to an something artificial that is used as a substitute for the genuine article. In "Choose Your Weapons," we learn that Otto was served actual coffee, while the other prisoners had to settle for "ersatz," probably something made from boiling grains and containing little or no actual coffee.

Gestapo – This was the commonly-used abbreviation for *Geheime Staatspolizei*, which translates to "Secret State Police" (of Nazi Germany).

ghetto – The ghetto was a section of a city in which Jews were forced to live. They were very densely populated, and those living within ghetto walls were subjected to severe conditions, economic restrictions, and tremendous hardship.

Götterdämmerung – In Norse mythology, this term referred to a cataclysmic battle between the gods of good and evil, preceding the destruction of the world. It was the title of an opera by Richard Wagner, the German composer. In "Follow Me Into Auschwitz," the term is used to refer to the German war effort.

jurisprudence – This is the philosophy, science, or practice of law.

kapo – This was the title given to a concentration camp prisoner given special privileges and comforts in exchange for overseeing prisoner work brigades. *Kapos* were often brutal toward fellow prisoners, trying to please their Nazi masters and maintain their advantage. In "Choose Your Weapons," David complains about Otto, a *kapo*, stealing other prisoners's food rations.

lieder – This is the plural form of the word lied (pronounced "leet"), the German word for "song." It generally refers to expressive German melodies from the 19th-century Romantic period. In "Concert at Auschwitz," the opera singer sings *lieder,* as demanded by the guard, Irma Grese.

Obersturmführerin – This is the female form of *Obersturmführer*, a Nazi paramilitary rank. It translates to "senior assault leader."

pogrom – This is an organized massacre of a particular ethnic group, usually referring to slaughter of European Jews. When concentration camp survivors learned of pogroms targeting those returning to their hometowns, many decided that it was unsafe to return to theirs.

SS – This is an abbreviation of *Schutzstaffel,* German for "Protective Echelon." The SS were the black-uniformed elite police and military corps of the Nazi movement.

Star of David – The Nazis identified Jews (and made it easy for them to be detected and ridiculed) by requiring them to wear a six-pointed yellow star. Jews would be severely punished if found in public without the star affixed to their clothing, both on the left breast and on the back.

swastika – An ancient symbol resembling a twisted cross. This became the emblem of the German Nazi party.

Träumerei – This is one of the best-known pieces written by German composer Robert Schumann. Translated into English, the word means "Dreaming."

tribunal – This is a body convened to make a legal inquiry or judgment. "Follow Me Into Auschwitz" mentions tribunals determining the guilt or innocence of Nazi leaders charged with crimes against humanity.

Acknowledgments

MANY PEOPLE ENCOURAGED AND SUPPORTED ME over the years it has taken to prepare this book for publication. The quality of my mother's writing intimidated me as I tried to write a foreword and afterword, and I knew nothing about publishing. I sincerely thank all those who spurred me on in a variety of ways as this precious book slowly, but surely, took shape.

My two writing coaches, Leslie Caplan and Paul Steinle, gave me courage to proceed. Leslie's writing prompts helped me reflect on my experiences as the child of Holocaust survivors and to put my thoughts on paper, scattered as they were. Paul sifted through years' worth of my ramblings, identifying and organizing excerpts that best captured what I wanted to say.

I experienced the power of my mother's stories when I read them in middle- and high-school classrooms. I am grateful to Bob Schug and Betsy Bishop (of Bentley School in Oakland, CA and Ashland High School in Ashland, OR respectively) for regularly inviting me into their classrooms. Their students' reactions (and sometimes those of parents who expressed interest after their children mentioned the stories at home), persuaded me to share Mom's stories with as wide an audience as possible.

Many friends have read and been moved by the stories. For their thoughtful feedback, I thank Dennis Read, Gary Goodman, Gail Offen-Brown, Susanne Severeid, Kenneth Ehrlich, Sharon Froba, Karen Peterson, Pat Conway, Sharon Jensen, Ron Mogel, Stephanie Stewart, Louis Pierotti, Udo and Sabina Gorsch-Nies, Maddalena DiRienzo, and Joan Ringelheim. I also acknowledge the many students who heard the stories and took the time to write heartfelt letters about how they were impacted by them. Such generously-offered commentary has been a precious gift. There are surely others who also deserve to be recognized, and I apologize to those I forgot to mention.

Special thanks to those who volunteered to write testimonial comments about the book. Some are identified above, but this group also includes George Conklin, Kathleen Cepelka, Dennis Eisner, Amanda Solomon, and Shannon Fleischman.

I am thankful to Doris Hobson for writing her letter to the Northern California History Project in 1992, documenting details about Holocaust experiences she overhead her parents and mine discussing. That letter, which I discovered in 2013, answered questions I had pondered for many years, specifically about the kind of work my parents did while struggling to stay alive in the camps. I am grateful that Doris's son, David Underwood, granted me permission to include her letter here.

Book designer Chris Molé has taken my simple typewritten manuscript and turned it into this graceful volume that would have made my stylish mother proud. I appreciate Chris's expertise, wisdom, and patience throughout this process.

A few months ago, my wife, Joanne Kliejunas, and I were ruminating about the important things we still wanted to accomplish in our lives. The completion of this book topped my list. Joanne knows how important my mother's stories are to me and supported my efforts throughout by offering constructive criticism of my drafts, helping me make key decisions, and providing sound (though not always easy to hear) advice.

Finally, I want to express gratitude to my parents, Abram and Felicia, and my late brother, Josef, who nurtured me, in spite of the grief associated with being a Holocaust-surviving family. I miss them tremendously and thank them for my cherished, joyful memories of our life together.

Made in the USA
Monee, IL
18 June 2023